Data Science and Analytics

Transforming Raw Data into Actionable Insights: A Comprehensive Guide

Marlowe Reyes

Table of Contents

INTRODUCTION

Learning to harness the power of data has become essential for both individuals and organizations in an era where it is being lauded as the new oil. This book, your comprehensive guide, not only provides a deep understanding of both fundamental ideas and innovative techniques but also equips you with the practical skills to navigate the ever-changing field of data science and analytics. Welcome to "Data Science and Analytics: Transforming Raw Data into Actionable Insights: A Comprehensive Guide."

This guide covers a wide range of subjects, from the fundamentals of data gathering and preprocessing to the complexities of machine learning and deep learning. You will delve into practical data visualization techniques, examine essential programs like R and Python, and discover how to apply analytics in various fields, including business, healthcare, finance, and marketing. Each topic is presented with a real-world context, making the learning experience more engaging and relevant.

This book also discusses the practical and ethical issues that arise from data science, providing insights into security, privacy, and moral decision-making. With the aid of real-world case studies, you can witness theory in action and close the knowledge gap between theory and practical application.

This thorough guide will give you the knowledge and resources to turn raw data into valuable insights, whether you're a student, an aspiring data scientist, or a seasoned expert looking to brush up on your craft. Set out on this adventure to become an expert in the science and art of making evidence-based decisions.

CHAPTER I

Understanding Data

Types of Data: Structured vs. Unstructured

The digital world relies heavily on data, which drives everything from scientific discoveries to corporate choices. Knowing the many types of data, especially structured and unstructured data, is essential for data science and analytics. Every type has unique traits, benefits, and difficulties, but both are essential for deriving significant insights.

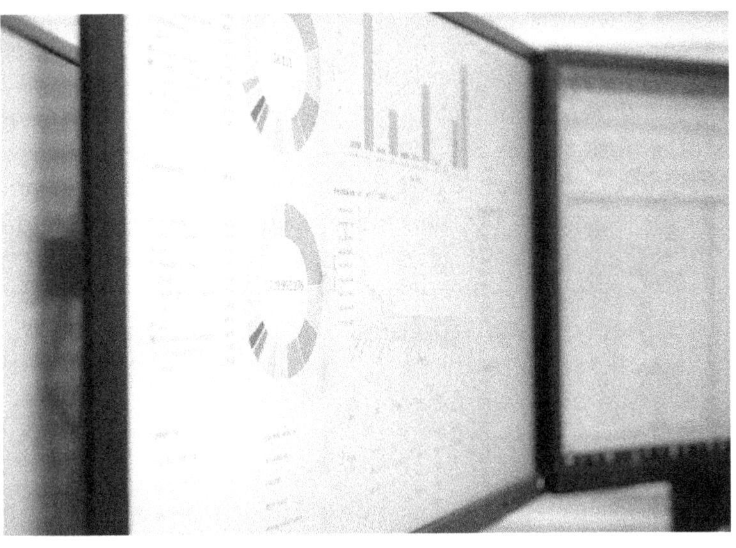

In databases, structured data stands as a beacon of reliability and efficiency. It is meticulously organized and straightforward to search, kept in fixed fields in records or files, often in spreadsheets or relational databases. Strings, dates, and numbers are a few examples that fit snugly into pre-made tables and schemas. The simplicity and usability of this data type are its shining attributes.

Structured data is accessible to evaluate with conventional data analysis tools and procedures because it is consistent and adheres to a predetermined format. As Structured Query Language (SQL) is so effective at managing these kinds of organized datasets, it is frequently used for managing and querying structured data. Financial reporting, inventory management, and customer relationship management (CRM) are just a few of the jobs that structured data excels at, instilling confidence in its dependability and efficiency.

Structured data has its limitations, though. Although it frequently necessitates extensive preprocessing to fit data into specified structures, its stringent format can be restrictive. This rigidity can make it more challenging to record the entire range of information that is accessible, especially in situations when the data is heterogeneous and does not follow a set structure.

Unstructured data, on the other hand, is a realm of complexity and intrigue. It is not based on any pre established model or schema and can take many different forms, including emails, text documents, photos, videos, posts on social media, and more. The bulk of data produced nowadays is of this kind, which reflects the range and complexity of information found in the actual world. Because unstructured data is disorganized, it is more difficult to examine by nature, often requiring the application of cutting-edge methods and tools, adding to its allure and challenge.

The heterogeneity of unstructured data is one of its main problems. Since the format and content of each unstructured data item might differ significantly, complex algorithms are needed to process and interpret the data in a meaningful way. In this field, Natural Language Processing (NLP) is a crucial technology that makes it possible to extract insights from textual data by processing human language in a form that computers can understand. Similarly, sophisticated machine learning models are needed for picture and video analysis to recognize patterns and interpret visual data.

Despite these obstacles, unstructured data has enormous insight potential. It offers a more complex picture of reality by bringing context and information-organized data to light. For example, customer sentiments, new trends, and user behaviors might be discovered through studying social media interactions, video footage, and customer reviews—things that structured data analysis alone could miss. Understanding human behavior and preferences is crucial in industries like marketing, healthcare, and the media, where the capacity to evaluate unstructured data is becoming increasingly important.

For data scientists, the integration of structured and unstructured data is a realm of endless possibilities. By combining the two, one can harness the advantages of each data type and produce a more thorough study. To provide a comprehensive picture of business success, unstructured consumer feedback insights can be added to organized transactional data. However, to achieve this integration, advanced data management techniques and systems that can handle a variety of data kinds are needed, inspiring data scientists to push the boundaries of their field.

In response to these difficulties, big data technologies—like Hadoop and Spark—have surfaced, offering frameworks for handling and storing massive amounts of heterogeneous data. Organizations may extract meaningful insights from their whole data landscape by using these technologies to make integrating and analyzing structured and unstructured data easier. To sum up, data science and analytics require organized and unstructured data to be effective. For tasks that call for accuracy and efficiency, structured data is essential due to its organization and simplicity of analysis. On the other hand, unstructured data captures the multidimensional quality of real-world information and delivers depth and richness despite its complexity. Data scientists may provide significant insights that support creative thinking and well-informed decision-making in various fields by comprehending and utilizing the advantages of both forms of data. The capacity to effectively combine and evaluate these many forms of data, realizing their full potential to convert unprocessed data into valuable insights, will determine the future direction of data science.

Data Sources and Collection Methods

The caliber and variety of data sources, along with the techniques used for data collection, are pivotal in the realm of data science and analytics. Data forms the bedrock for analysis, insights, and decision-making. For a data scientist to effectively transform raw data into actionable insights, it is imperative to have a comprehensive grasp of the diverse data sources and collection techniques that are constantly evolving in this field.

Data sources for data science and analytics can be broadly categorized into primary and secondary sources. Secondary data, which is pre-existing information collected for other purposes but can be reused for fresh analysis, and primary data, which is first-hand information gathered specifically for a particular study, each have their own unique advantages and challenges.

Most primary data sources are gathered using direct interactions with participants or systems. Surveys are a popular technique that asks respondents a series of questions to learn more about their attitudes, behaviors, and other traits. Researchers can customize survey questions to suit their needs by administering them in person, over the phone, or online. Experiments are another technique in which researchers change one or more parameters and track how those changes affect a dependent variable. When establishing causality in controlled conditions, this approach is constructive. Observational studies are another primary technique for gathering data, which entails methodically documenting actions or occurrences as they happen naturally and unhindered. Real-time phenomenon analysis is an everyday use of this approach in the social sciences and medical fields.

Existing datasets that were gathered for other objectives but might be used for fresh analysis are examples of secondary data sources. These sources are numerous and diverse; they include information from commercial companies like sales records, customer databases, transactional data, and information from government databases like economic statistics and census data. Secondary data can be found on open data platforms and academic research libraries. When weighed against the expense and ease of access, these sources provide much information that cannot be obtained through primary data collection.

The emergence of big data has brought new and varied data streams in addition to these conventional data sources. For example, social media networks produce enormous volumes of data every day. Social media platforms like Facebook, Instagram, and Twitter offer diverse datasets comprising text, photographs, videos, and user interactions. These datasets enable real-time insights about user sentiments, trends, and behaviors. Another method of getting data from websites is web scraping. Many data are gathered from online sources, including product reviews, news stories, and forum conversations, utilizing automated technologies. Continuous data streams are also produced by IoT (Internet of Things) devices from sensors installed in various contexts, such as wearable technology, smart homes, and industrial systems. For predictive analytics and monitoring, this real-time data is priceless.

In the digital age, data collection techniques have advanced significantly. Adopting APIs (Application Programming Interfaces), which enable smooth data interchange across systems, is one crucial breakthrough. APIs make it easier for data scientists to integrate disparate data sources by giving them access to real-time data from various platforms, including social media, financial markets, and weather services. Using cloud based data collection systems, which offer scalable options for gathering and storing big datasets, is an additional technique. With the help of these technologies, data may be processed, gathered from many sources, and safely stored in cloud environments.

Despite the large number of data sources and collection techniques, several issues remain. Ensuring data correctness, consistency, and completeness is essential for trustworthy analysis, making it the top priority. Data security and privacy are also significant concerns, especially when handling sensitive data. Data-gathering procedures must be guided by ethical considerations to uphold confidence and safeguard individual rights.

In summary, the field of data science and analytics has access to a wide range of data sources and gathering techniques that are constantly changing. Primary and secondary data sources and contemporary digital data streams like social media and Internet of Things devices provide rich datasets that support analysis and insights. Data collection techniques are varied and ever more complex, ranging from tests and surveys to web scraping and API integration. Data scientists who want to utilize data fully must understand these sources and techniques to ensure that the conclusions drawn are accurate, trustworthy, and morally sound. Gaining proficiency in these areas will promote innovation and produce significant results across various industries as data becomes increasingly important in decision-making and technology develops.

Data Quality and Integrity

The ideas of data integrity and quality are crucial in the fields of analytics and data science. Data integrity guarantees that information is accurate, consistent, and trustworthy throughout its lifecycle, while high-quality data is the foundation of trustworthy insights and sound decision-making. To obtain relevant results and actionable insights, it is crucial to comprehend and preserve the integrity and quality of data.

Data state based on elements like correctness, completeness, dependability, and relevance is data quality. Valid analyses depend on accurate data accurately reflecting the values it represents in the real world. For example, proper diagnostic and treatment recommendations in healthcare analytics depend on reliable patient data. To be complete, one must possess every information needed to examine thoroughly. Inaccurate judgments and skewed outcomes might arise from missing data. Data consistency throughout time and across several datasets is referred to as reliability. Longitudinal studies and trend analyses are made more accessible by reliable data, guaranteeing that the same data points are consistent across different systems and periods. Relevance is the degree to which the data apply to the particular requirements of the analysis. Significant patterns can be obscured and noise introduced by irrelevant data.

On the other hand, maintaining and guaranteeing the quality and consistency of data across its whole lifecycle is known as data integrity. This includes entering, storing, transferring, and retrieving data. Information must be protected from tampering, illegal access, and other threats to ensure data integrity. Validation, which involves comparing data to predetermined standards and guidelines to ensure it satisfies requirements before being utilized in analysis, is a crucial component of data integrity. Logical consistency checks, format checks, and range checks are examples of this. Future dates, for instance, should not appear in a birthdate field, and numerical fields ought to be within acceptable bounds.

Maintaining data integrity and quality presents several issues, particularly in light of the massive volumes of data produced in the current digital era. Data duplication, or recording the same data point more than once in several systems, is a significant problem. It may result in disparities and inconsistencies that distort the analysis's findings. Data corruption is another problem arising during data storage or transport due to hostile attacks, software defects, or hardware malfunctions. Corrupt data may compromise the entire dataset, making it unusable.

Another critical component influencing data quality is human error. Mistakes such as typos or improper data coding can introduce inaccuracies during data entry. These mistakes are prevalent in manual data entry procedures and can build up over time to cause a significant deterioration in quality. Furthermore, there may be difficulties in integrating data from various sources. Several systems' standards, formats, and definitions differ, making the consolidation process more difficult and potentially resulting in misunderstandings or loss of data integrity.

Organizations use a range of tactics and technologies to address these issues. Finding and fixing mistakes and inconsistencies in data is a crucial step in improving its quality, which is known as data cleaning or cleansing. This can involve standardizing formats, eliminating duplicates, and fixing errors. Automated tools and algorithms can aid this process, increasing its accuracy and efficiency.

Data governance frameworks are necessary to preserve data integrity and quality. These frameworks set standards, guidelines, and practices for data management throughout an enterprise. Effective data governance lowers the possibility of errors and inconsistencies by ensuring that data is handled, processed, and stored consistently in accordance with best practices. Providing responsibility and ongoing oversight also entails designating positions inside the business with specific data quality and integrity duties.

Technology-based solutions are essential for ensuring the integrity of data. Transaction management is one of the services offered by database management systems (DBMS), which guarantees that all data activities are carried out accurately and completely. These systems can prevent corruption by returning to the most recent consistent state during an interruption. Data is shielded from manipulation and unwanted access via encryption and access controls, guaranteeing that only authorized users can read or alter the data.

In summary, the effectiveness of data science and analytics depends critically on the quality and integrity of the data. Reliable, thorough, accurate, and pertinent data is the foundation for insightful conclusions that may be put into practice. Data integrity guarantees that this information is free from corruption and unwanted access and is consistent and reliable throughout its lifecycle. To tackle the problems related to data quality and integrity, a comprehensive set of procedures, efficient governance, and cutting-edge technology solutions are needed. Organizations can improve the dependability of their data and, as a result, make better decisions and provide more meaningful results from their analytical activities by prioritizing these factors.

CHAPTER II

Fundamental Concepts

Statistics for Data Science

Statistics is not just a theoretical concept, but a practical tool in the world of data science and analytics. It equips us with the necessary instruments to comprehend, evaluate, and interpret data, making it a fundamental aspect of these fields. By turning raw data into usable insights, statistics plays a crucial role in various domains where data science is gaining prominence.

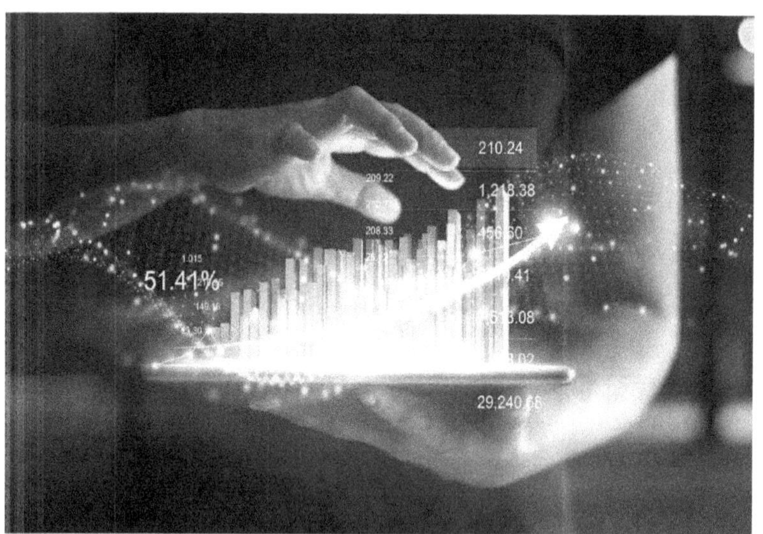

At its core, statistics is about more than just numbers. It's about gathering, analyzing, interpreting, presenting, and organizing data. This process enables data scientists to extract and summarize significant patterns and insights from massive amounts of data, making sense of the information. Descriptive statistics, for instance, provide a description of a dataset's primary characteristics, including metrics like mean, median, mode, variance, and standard deviation. These measurements are the first step in any data analysis process, helping us understand the data's central tendency, dispersion, and overall distribution.

Using sample data to make predictions or inferences about the population, inferential statistics broadens the use of descriptive statistics. This statistical feature is essential to data science because it permits generalizations beyond the current dataset as it facilitates prediction-making and decision-making under uncertainty. Inferential statistics relies heavily on regression analysis, confidence intervals, and hypothesis testing. Confidence intervals offer a range of values within which a population parameter is predicted to lay with a certain degree of confidence. In contrast, hypothesis testing, for instance, assists in determining whether a particular assumption about a dataset is valid.

In data science, regression analysis—single and multiple —is especially important for modeling relationships between variables. A single independent variable is utilized in simple linear regression, which uses the linear connection between the two variables to predict the value of a dependent variable. In contrast, multiple regression incorporates several independent variables and yields a more intricate model that may explain the combined effects and interactions of various factors on a dependent variable. Regression analysis is a crucial predictive modeling component because it enables data scientists to project future patterns and behaviors from past data.

Probability theory is a crucial component of statistics in data science. Most real-world data scenarios contain some degree of uncertainty, which may be quantified mathematically using probability. Modeling random variables and their behaviors requires understanding probability distributions, such as the Poisson, binomial, and normal distributions. These distributions are essential to many statistical techniques, such as hypothesis testing and Bayesian analysis, and aid in evaluating the likelihood of various events.

Based on Bayes' theorem, Bayesian statistics provides a potent method for revising a hypothesis's probability as new data or evidence becomes available. In data science, this approach is constructive for creating more resilient and adaptable models that can account for past information and adjust to fresh data. Various applications, such as machine learning, use Bayesian inference to build probabilistic models that improve with more data.

Statistics and machine learning are not separate entities, but interconnected fields. In fact, statistical principles are the foundation of many machine-learning approaches. For example, statistical approaches are used by classification algorithms such as logistic regression and support vector machines to classify data points into predetermined classes. Clustering algorithms, including k-means and hierarchical clustering, group similar data points together based on statistical measurements of similarity or distance. This integration of statistics and machine learning is a testament to the importance of statistics in data science and analytics.

Principal component analysis (PCA) and other dimensionality reduction techniques employ statistical techniques to minimize the number of variables in a dataset while maintaining most of the variation, simplifying the study without sacrificing important information. These methods are essential for managing high-dimensional data, prevalent in contemporary datasets, and enhancing machine learning models' effectiveness and performance.

In summary, statistics plays a crucial role in data science and analytics by offering the frameworks and procedures required for gathering, analyzing, and interpreting data. While inferential statistics enable predictions and generalizations, descriptive statistics provide fundamental data comprehension. The mathematical foundations for modeling uncertainty and updating beliefs with new knowledge are offered by probability theory and Bayesian statistics. These methods are used by machine learning, which has its roots in statistical concepts, to create prediction models and draw conclusions from large, complicated datasets. To fully utilize data and support well-informed decision-making across various industries, a data scientist must possess a solid statistical understanding.

Probability Theory

Probability theory is an optional skill for data scientists and analysts and a fundamental field element. It offers the mathematical framework for comprehending and measuring uncertainty, serving as the foundation for statistical inference. It empowers data scientists to test theories, make predictions, and create models that accurately capture the intricacies of the real world. Any data scientist who wants to draw valuable conclusions from data and make defensible judgments based on those conclusions must grasp probability theory. Understanding probability theory is not just beneficial but necessary for success in the field of data science and analytics.

Probability theory is concerned with the possibility that occurrences will occur. It offers a systematic approach to reasoning about the uncertainty and randomness included in data. Probability measures, occurrences, results, and experiments are the fundamental components of probability theory. Any process with a specified set of possible outcomes that may be repeated indefinitely is considered an experiment. For instance, an experiment with six possible results is rolling a dice. An event is a subset of the sample space or the set of all possible outcomes. Each event is given a numerical value by probability measures, which express the possibility of the event occurring.

The probability distribution is a fundamental idea in probability theory that explains the distribution of probabilities among various outcomes in a sample space. Probability distributions come in diverse varieties, each with unique uses and functions. Countable outcomes, like the roll of a die or the quantity of faulty items in a batch, are covered by the discrete probability distribution. For instance, the binomial distribution describes the number of successes in a predetermined number of independent trials, each with an equal chance of success. In risk assessment and quality control, this distribution is frequently utilized.

Conversely, continuous probability distributions handle situations when the possible outcomes fall within a constant range of values. The most well-known continuous distribution is the normal distribution, sometimes called the Gaussian distribution. Its symmetrical bell-shaped curve around the mean is what makes it unique. In data science, the normal distribution is widely used to model variables such as measurement mistakes and natural occurrences. It is a fundamental component of many statistical approaches. The exponential and Poisson distributions, which represent the interval between events and count data, are two other significant continuous distributions.

Conditional probability and independence are two essential ideas in probability theory that significantly impact data science. The chance of an event happening in the presence of another event that has already happened is known as conditional probability. It is necessary to comprehend how variables relate to one another and build models considering these dependencies. Conversely, independence suggests that the likelihood of one event occurring does not change when another happens. These ideas form the basis of Bayesian statistics, which modifies a hypothesis's probability in response to new information.

Based on Bayes' theorem, Bayesian statistics is a potent method in probability theory. It offers a structure for revising a hypothesis's likelihood in light of fresh information. The Bayes theorem relates the conditional and marginal probability of random events, which makes it possible to include past knowledge in the analysis. In data science, this method is beneficial for creating probabilistic models that can learn from data and improve over time. Bayesian techniques are used in many fields, such as machine learning, where they aid in creating models that are more predictive and adaptive to new data.

In probability theory, random variables and their anticipated values are also essential ideas—a random variable changes in value according to how a random event turns out. The long-term average value of a random variable that measures the central tendency is called the expected value or mean. The spread or dispersion of a random variable is measured by variance and standard deviation, which show how far the values differ from the mean. These metrics are essential for comprehending data distribution and behavior and important for determining risk and making decisions.

Probability theory is the foundation for many models and algorithms used in data science to analyze data. For example, Naive Bayes and other classification algorithms classify data points according to their attributes using probability. Clustering techniques, such as Gaussian Mixture Models, use probability distributions to group related data points. Probability theory aids in proactive decision-making in predictive modeling by estimating the chance of future events based on historical evidence. Probability theory is not just a tool but a key to unlocking the potential of data science and analytics. It provides the frameworks and instruments required to manage uncertainty, forecast outcomes, and create reliable models. Understanding probability distributions, conditional probability, independence, Bayesian statistics, and random variable behavior not only enhances data interpretation and analysis skills but also serves as the foundation for the creation of models and algorithms that convert raw, unprocessed data into meaningful insights. As data continues to rise in volume and complexity, probability theory will play an increasingly important role in guiding data-driven decisions, underscoring its power and potential in the field of data science.

Hypothesis Testing and Inferential Statistics

In data science and analytics, hypothesis testing and inferential statistics are fundamental ideas that offer crucial instruments for making inferences about populations from sample data. Using these techniques, data scientists can test hypotheses, draw conclusions, and assess the importance of links found in data. In particular, hypothesis testing is a systematic process determining whether there is sufficient data to reject a null hypothesis in favor of an alternative hypothesis. The alternative hypothesis typically represents the researcher's assertion or the existence of an effect, whereas the null hypothesis usually represents the status quo or a lack of effect. A formal foundation for decision making and population-related inferences is provided by hypothesis testing, which compares sample statistics to theoretical distributions under the null hypothesis.

The t-test, which compares the means of two groups, is one of the most widely used methods in hypothesis testing. To determine whether there is a significant difference in the average salary between two departments in a corporation, for instance, a t-test might be utilized. The chi-squared test, another popular technique, evaluates the relationship between categorical variables. This test could determine whether voting preferences in an election are significantly influenced by gender. These tests offer a systematic way to assess theories and draw conclusions about the population using sample data.

Using a sample of data, inferential statistics expands on the concepts of hypothesis testing to generate predictions or conclusions about the population. With this method, data scientists can extrapolate results from the current dataset to more significant phenomena and make conclusions. Confidence intervals are standard in inferential statistics, which give a range of values within which a population parameter is predicted to reside with a particular degree of confidence. For instance, a population's mean salary with a 95% confidence interval would signify that we have 95% confidence that the genuine mean is within the given range. Confidence intervals are a helpful tool for decision-making and provide a more sophisticated understanding of the inherent uncertainty in statistical findings.

Another effective method in inferential statistics is regression analysis, which enables data scientists to model correlations between variables and generate predictions based on those correlations. One way to investigate the linear relationship between a dependent variable and one independent variable is by simple linear regression. For example, this technique may forecast home values based on square footage. This method can be expanded to include numerous independent variables using multiple regression, enabling a more complicated model to account for the combined effects of various factors on a dependent variable. Using regression analysis, data scientists can determine significant predictors, evaluate the direction and strength of correlations, and create well-informed forecasts based on observed data.

A flexible method of inference that takes into account past knowledge and modifies beliefs in light of new information is provided by Bayesian statistics. This approach is constructive for modeling uncertainty and creating predictions in dynamic contexts in data science. Data scientists may create probabilistic models with Bayesian inference that adjust to new data and produce increasingly accurate estimates over time. For instance, stock price forecasts based on historical data and the most recent developments in the market and economy might be made using Bayesian approaches. Bayesian statistics helps data scientists make better decisions and get better results from their analysis by utilizing past information and repeatedly updating beliefs.

In summary, inferential statistics and hypothesis testing are crucial instruments in data science and analytics because they enable inferences about populations from sample data. Data scientists can test theories, forecast outcomes, and extrapolate results beyond the scope of the current dataset using these techniques. Utilizing methods like chi-squared tests, regression analysis, confidence intervals, t-tests, and Bayesian inference, data scientists can find significant associations, unearth insightful information, and make defensible conclusions based on empirical evidence. As data science advances and becomes more prevalent across different fields, a firm grasp of hypothesis testing and inferential statistics will be necessary to generate actionable insights and spur innovation.

CHAPTER III

Data Processing

Data Cleaning and Preprocessing

Preparation and data cleansing are essential processes in the workflow of data science and analytics. These procedures guarantee that the data is reliable, consistent, and appropriate for the intended application for analysis and model creation. The validity and dependability of the insights drawn from data are strongly influenced by its quality, which is why data cleaning and preprocessing are crucial for successful data science.

Data cleaning is known as finding and fixing mistakes and inconsistencies within the dataset. This phase is essential because raw data frequently contains errors, missing values, and duplicate entries. These problems can have several causes, such as inaccuracies in human data entry, flawed data gathering procedures, or system malfunctions. Usually, missing value detection and management come first when cleaning data. In certain situations, statistical imputation techniques like mean or median imputation or more complex methods like regression imputation can be used to attribute missing variables. Alternatively, if they jeopardize the dataset's integrity, rows or columns with a high percentage of missing data may be eliminated.

Another prevalent problem in raw data is outliers. These data points show a significant deviation from the rest of the dataset, which may cause bias in the results or point to mistakes in the data collection process. Several statistical techniques, including z-score analysis and the interquartile range (IQR) method, can be used to identify outliers. Depending on their nature and the context of the analysis, outliers can be dealt with by deleting or altering them after they have been detected.

Data preparation entails converting unprocessed data into a format that can be analyzed, going beyond superficial cleaning. This stage involves feature engineering, encoding categorical variables, normalization, and standardization. Numerical data is normalized to a range, usually between 0 and 1, which is helpful when the data is going to be used in algorithms like neural networks that are sensitive to the scale of the input data. In contrast, standardization yields a zero mean and one standard deviation, which is helpful for algorithms like logistic regression and support vector machines.

Another crucial preprocessing step is encoding categorical variables. Because categorical data has qualitative qualities, it needs to be transformed into a numerical format to be utilized by most machine learning algorithms. This can be accomplished using methods like label encoding, which gives each category a unique integer, or one-hot encoding, which generates binary columns for each category. Every approach has advantages and disadvantages, and the selection is based on the analysis's particular needs and the algorithms employed.

The act of developing new features from the available data to capture the underlying relationships and patterns more effectively is known as feature engineering. This may entail generating new measurements that offer more insights, merging already-existing features, or developing interaction words. By giving machine learning models more pertinent data, efficient feature engineering can dramatically improve their performance.

Preprocessing and data cleansing are iterative procedures that call for in-depth knowledge of the data and topic expertise. When new information becomes available or the data changes, the process frequently needs to be repeated and improved. Automated tools and libraries support these activities, such as R's dplyr and Tidy, Python's Pandas, and Scikit-learn, allowing data scientists to clean and preprocess big datasets effectively.

Data cleaning and preprocessing, despite the availability of technologies, remain labor-intensive processes that require meticulous attention to detail. The decisions made by data scientists during these phases can significantly impact the analysis and the conclusions derived from the data. This underscores the crucial role of data scientists in the data science endeavor, making them feel valued and integral to the process. A clean, consistent, and well-preprocessed dataset, a result of their diligent work, is the cornerstone of any successful data science endeavor.

To sum everything up, preprocessing and data cleansing are essential steps in the data science and analytics workflow. To obtain trustworthy and significant insights, they ensure the data is correct, consistent, and prepared for analysis. These procedures need value handling, outlier detection and handling, data normalization and standardization, categorical variable encoding, and feature engineering. Tools and libraries can help with these activities, but they must be done carefully and with subject knowledge. Data scientists can significantly improve the caliber and efficacy of their models and analyses by devoting time and resources to comprehensive data cleaning and preprocessing, resulting in more reliable conclusions and better decision making.

Handling Missing Values

In the realm of data science and analytics, the importance of handling missing values cannot be overstated. Incomplete data can significantly undermine the accuracy and dependability of analysis, as well as the performance of models. The methods used to address missing values are diverse, depending on the type of data, the quantity of missing data, and the underlying causes of their absence. It's crucial to remember that a robust dataset, free from missing values, is the foundation for accurate and dependable insights.

Missing data can stem from various sources, such as non responses in surveys, human errors in data entry, and system failures. The first step in addressing missing data is to grasp its pattern and mechanism. There are three types of missing data: Missing Not at Random (MNAR), Missing Completely at Random (MCAR), and Missing at Random (MAR). Understanding these types is crucial as it helps in selecting the most appropriate approach to handle them, underscoring the complexity and depth of the issue.

Deleted rows or columns with missing values are removed from the dataset as a common method of handling missing values. This approach is straightforward, but if missing values are common, it can result in significant data loss, mainly when listwise deletion is used to remove complete rows with any missing values. While pairwise deletion can reduce some data loss, it can also introduce biases and inconsistencies because it uses all available data without discarding entire rows.

Another popular method for dealing with missing values is imputation, which substitutes predicted values for the missing data. The observed data's mean, median, or mode are substituted for the missing values in simple imputation techniques, such as mean, median, or mode imputation. These techniques are simple, but they could produce skewed estimates since they need to consider the variability in the data. Regression imputation, which predicts missing values using a regression model based on other factors in the dataset, and k-nearest neighbors (KNN) imputation, which estimates missing values based on the nearest data points, are examples of more sophisticated imputation techniques.

Using a sophisticated approach called multiple imputations, repeatedly imputed missing values create numerous plausible datasets, and each is analyzed independently before the results are combined. This approach yields more precise and trustworthy estimates by considering the missing data's uncertainty. Multiple imputation is especially helpful when working with massive datasets that include intricate patterns of missingness.

Machine learning methods can also handle missing values. Missing data can be handled by techniques like decision trees and random forests by treating the missingness as an extra characteristic. Furthermore, the accuracy of the imputations is increased by iterative imputation techniques like the Expectation-Maximization (EM) algorithm, which iteratively predicts missing values based on maximum likelihood estimations.

The context and analysis objectives determine the best approach for managing missing values. Sometimes, missing data might provide crucial information, and figuring out the pattern of missingness can yield insightful information. For example, if some survey responses are consistently absent, this may point to a more severe problem that has to be fixed. Therefore, before choosing an imputation approach, a thorough exploratory data analysis (EDA) is essential to determine the quantity and nature of missing values.

In real life, several steps are involved in managing missing values. To ensure that the chosen strategy does not add appreciable biases or skew the findings, data scientists frequently experiment with several approaches and confirm their findings. Data cleaning is made more accessible by the comprehensive features provided by tools and libraries like Scikit-learn, R's mouse package, and Python's Pandas, which can be used to identify, analyze, and impute missing values.

In conclusion, managing missing values is a cornerstone of analytics and data science. It's not just a necessary step, but a strategic one that can significantly enhance the quality of analysis and model performance. The strategies for handling missing values are diverse, ranging from basic imputation and deletion to advanced machine learning and multiple imputation. The type of data, the missingness pattern, and the specific analysis objectives all play a role in method selection. By mastering the art of handling missing values, data scientists can ensure the accuracy and dependability of their datasets, leading to more impactful and precise insights.

Data Transformation and Normalization

In data science and analytics, data transformation and normalization are essential procedures that guarantee data is in an appropriate format for modeling and analysis. These procedures improve the data's quality, dependability, and interpretability, allowing analysts to derive more precise and significant conclusions.

Converting data from one format or structure to another is known as data transformation. This stage is crucial because unprocessed data gathered from multiple sources frequently has errors, missing values, and inconsistent formats, making analysis difficult. Numerous methods, including feature engineering, integration, reduction, and data cleaning, are used in the transformation process. Data cleaning deals with faults and inconsistencies in the data by fixing mistakes, getting rid of duplicates, and managing missing numbers. Whereas reduction strategies concentrate on streamlining the dataset by eliminating redundant information and lowering its dimensionality, integration entails merging data from several sources to produce a cohesive view. Feature engineering is a technique used to improve the predictive value of data by adding new characteristics or altering preexisting ones.

Scaling data to a conventional range or distribution is referred to as normalization, a subset of data transformation. It is especially crucial for machine learning methods like neural networks and k-nearest neighbors (KNN), which are sensitive to the volume of input data. Different normalization strategies best serve various types of data and analysis requirements. By rescaling the data to a predetermined range, usually 0 to 1, min-max scaling, for example, guarantees that each feature contributes equally to the study. Z-score normalization is another popular technique that turns data into a distribution with a mean of 0 and a standard deviation of 1 by standardizing it according to its mean and standard deviation. This approach works particularly well in cases where the data has a Gaussian distribution.

Data transformation and normalization are essential to get data ready for analysis and machine learning. By guaranteeing that features are comparable and lowering the possibility of biases resulting from different data scales, properly transformed and normalized data enhance the performance of machine learning models. For instance, characteristics like square footage and the number of bedrooms may have wildly disparate ranges in a dataset containing home pricing information. Without normalization, algorithms could slant the analysis by favoring the feature with the more comprehensive numerical range. The model can learn more efficiently because every feature contributes equally when the data is normalized.

Data transformation and normalization also significantly enhance the interpretability of results. When the data is normalized, it becomes easier to compare and understand how different features influence the model's predictions. For example, in regression analysis, the coefficients of standardized features can be directly compared to determine their relative importance. This clarity in understanding can lead to better strategic planning and decision-making, as stakeholders can quickly identify the most significant elements.

Data transformation and standardization also make improved data visualization possible. Normalized data can enhance the clarity and efficacy of visual representations since visualization tools frequently presume that the data is in a standard format and range. After the data has been appropriately normalized, for example, scatter plots, histograms, and heatmaps can more precisely depict the relationships and distributions within the data.

Data transformation and normalization become even more crucial in the context of big data and real-time analytics. The sheer volume, variety, and velocity of data generated today necessitate robust transformation and normalization techniques. To handle and analyze data efficiently, automated tools and sophisticated algorithms are often used. These tools and algorithms are designed to manage these processes at scale and ensure that data is consistently ready for real-time analysis and decision making.

To sum up, data transformation and normalization are fundamental processes in the data science workflow that greatly influence the caliber and suitability of data for machine learning and analysis. These procedures ensure clean, consistent, and suitably scaled data, which improves decision-making and produces more accurate models and insights. Effective data transformation and normalization will become increasingly crucial as data grows in volume and complexity, highlighting their vital significance in data science and analytics.

CHAPTER IV

Programming for Data Science

Introduction to Python and R

In data science and analytics, Python and R are two of the most essential programming languages, each with unique advantages. Their broad industry acceptance is fueled by their vital ecosystems, extensive libraries, and capacity to manage various data-related tasks. Comprehending the functions, benefits, and synergies of R and Python in data science can significantly expand a data scientist's toolbox.

Python is a high-level, general-purpose programming language that was developed by Guido van Rossum and initially made available in 1991. It is renowned for being easily readable. Its simple, easy-to-understand syntax makes it suitable for novice users while retaining sufficient capability for more experienced users. Python is unparalleled in its adaptability within the field of data science. It is employed in web construction, data analysis, machine learning, and manipulation. The language's vast libraries provide a solid basis for data analysis jobs, including NumPy for numerical computations, Pandas for data manipulation, and Matplotlib for data visualization. Furthermore, the sci-kit-learn, TensorFlow, and Keras libraries for Python are crucial resources for putting machine learning and deep learning models into practice. Python's status as a mainstay in the data science process is further cemented by the ease with which it connects with other languages and platforms.

R is a programming language intended primarily for statistical computing and graphics. Ross Ihaka and Robert Gentleman created it and published it in 1995. Because of its data analysis-focused syntax and features, statisticians and data scientists who work on statistical modeling and data visualization frequently choose it. Thousands of packages are available in R's vast package ecosystem, especially the CRAN library, to expand its capabilities in graphical representations and statistical techniques. Using programs such as ggplot2, R can produce publication-quality graphics, making it an excellent tool for complex and adaptable visualizations. R becomes very useful in presenting statistical results and conducting exploratory data analysis. R is also vital for in-depth data analysis because of its built-in functions for statistical testing, linear and nonlinear modeling, and time-series analysis.

Even though Python and R both offer unique benefits, they are frequently combined to maximize their complementary qualities. Python's versatility makes it perfect for preprocessing, automating, and integrating data workflows, whereas R is more effective in statistical analysis and visualization in data science activities. For instance, a data scientist may utilize R for in-depth statistical analysis and produce excellent visualizations after using Python to clean and preprocess a sizable dataset and apply machine learning techniques. Tools like RPy2, which permits the integration of R within Python scripts, and the reticulate package, which enables the usage of Python within R, help to achieve this interoperability. With the help of these technologies, data scientists may take full advantage of the advantages of both languages without jumping between tools or contexts.

The decision between R and Python is frequently influenced by the type of analysis being done, the user's level of language proficiency, and the project's particular requirements. Python is a preferred language for activities requiring integration with databases, web applications, or the deployment of machine learning models due to its wide range of applications. For those new to programming, its comprehensive documentation and user-friendly syntax make it easy to learn. However, because of its emphasis on statistical analysis and robust visualization features, R is an excellent option for bioinformatics, academic research, and any other discipline that needs precise statistical analysis and concise, understandable data presentation.

To sum up, Python and R are essential languages in analytics and data science. Python benefits many data related activities, including web development, machine learning, and data cleaning. Its broad library support further contributes to its versatility. R is recommended for in-depth data analysis and visualization due to its advanced graphical tools and specialized statistical capabilities. A thorough understanding of using both languages efficiently can lead to a comprehensive and potent approach to data science, facilitating deeper insights and more productive workflows. Through the way Python and R work together, data scientists can take advantage of the most outstanding features of both languages and have the tools they need to handle the wide range of problems related to data analysis and interpretation.

Key Libraries and Packages

Using strong libraries and packages is crucial for effective data manipulation, analysis, visualization, and modeling in the quickly developing fields of data science and analytics. These tools offer robust functionality, simplify workflows, and make it easier for data scientists to tackle challenging jobs. Several essential libraries and packages have come to be considered necessary in the data science ecosystem, each providing exceptional capabilities suited to different facets of data science and analytics.

Pandas, a versatile Python library, is a cornerstone of data science. Its high-performance, user-friendly data structures, particularly DataFrames, are essential for data manipulation and analysis. Pandas's flexible features make data cleansing, transformation, and aggregation a breeze. It can read and write data from various file types, including SQL databases, Excel, and CSV files. Pandas is an indispensable tool for exploratory data analysis and preprocessing, thanks to its ability to manage missing data, combine datasets, and perform group operations.

Another fundamental library that's typically utilized for math operations is called NumPy. It enables effective mathematical and statistical processes by supporting matrices, arrays, and many mathematical functions. Many other scientific libraries are built around NumPy's array objects, which provide adequate storage and quick operations on big datasets. It is an essential library for scientific computing and data research because of its abilities in Fourier transforms, random number generation, and linear algebra.

Matplotlib and Seaborn are two of the most popular libraries for data visualization. Python users may create static, interactive, and animated visualizations with Matplotlib, a flexible charting package. Its wide variety of plot styles, which include scatter, line, bar, and histogram plots, provide intricate and adaptable data display. Seaborn provides a high-level interface for creating visually appealing and educational statistical visualizations. It is developed on top of Matplotlib. It makes it simpler to create intricate visualizations, such as violin plots, pair plots, and heatmaps, which facilitates the understanding and interpreting data linkages and patterns.

One notable library in machine learning is Scikit-learn, which offers easy-to-use data mining and analysis tools. Different machine learning algorithms for dimensionality reduction, clustering, regression, and classification are supported. Scikit-learn is accessible to novice and expert data scientists due to its user-friendly API, comprehensive documentation, and numerous examples. Workflows are made more accessible by their interface with other libraries, like NumPy and Pandas, which provide smooth transitions from feature selection and preprocessing to model evaluation and deployment.

TensorFlow and PyTorch are the two most popular frameworks for deep learning. Google has created a feature-rich open-source machine learning framework called TensorFlow. It offers an adaptable ecosystem of community resources, libraries, and tools to facilitate creating and applying machine learning models. TensorFlow may be used for a wide range of tasks, from straightforward neural networks to intricate multi-layered structures, thanks to its support for low-level operations and high-level APIs like Keras. Another well-liked deep learning framework is PyTorch, created by Facebook's AI Research group and renowned for its user-friendliness and dynamic computation graph. PyTorch is the recommended option for deep learning research and development because of its user-friendly interface and robust support for GPU acceleration.

Building upon NumPy, SciPy is another essential library that offers a variety of functions and algorithms for scientific and technical computing. It includes modules for eigenvalue problems, interpolation, optimization, integration, and other sophisticated mathematical operations. Due to its capacity to manage large-scale scientific computations, SciPy is a necessary library for many scientific applications.

The last essential tool in the data science toolbox is Jupyter Notebooks. These notebooks provide an interactive environment for data scientists to write and run code, display data, and record their workflows in a single, coherent document. Jupyter Notebooks are famous for sharing and presenting data science projects, and they support multiple computer languages, such as Python, R, and Julia.

In conclusion, the bedrock of data science and analytics is formed by essential libraries and packages including TensorFlow, NumPy, Matplotlib, Seaborn, Scikit-learn, PyTorch, SciPy, and Jupyter Notebooks. These tools, with their extensive features, empower data scientists to manage complex tasks and extract valuable insights from data by streamlining data manipulation, visualization, and modeling. As the discipline of data science continues to evolve, the growth and improvement of these libraries will be pivotal in expanding data science's capabilities and applications, and you, as a data scientist, are at the forefront of this exciting journey.

Writing Efficient Code

Writing efficient code is essential in data science and analytics, where processing massive amounts of data quickly and accurately can substantially impact the quality of insights and decision-making. Long-term projects require scalability, readability, and maintainability, all of which are ensured by efficient code in addition to improving performance. Data scientists may develop more effective code, more efficiently utilize computational resources, and enhance productivity by adhering to a few fundamental ideas and practices.

Optimization is one of the core ideas of effective coding. Selecting the appropriate algorithms and data structures is necessary to reduce memory consumption and computational complexity. Large datasets are best handled by algorithms with lower temporal complexity, such as those with logarithmic or linear performance. Similarly, code performance can be significantly improved using correct data structures, such as lists for ordered collections or dictionaries for quick lookups. Decisions about which algorithms and data structures to use must be well-informed and balanced to maximize efficiency.

Another essential tool for producing effective code is vectorization, especially for data science applications requiring numerical calculations. With vectorization, operations on entire arrays or matrices can be performed simultaneously without explicit loops, which are sometimes slow in high-level programming languages like Python. Instead, low-level, efficient implementations are utilized. Vectorized functions, which are substantially quicker than typical loops performing element-wise operations across arrays and Data Frames, are available in libraries like NumPy and Pandas. This results in more understandable and compact code while also accelerating computations.

Advanced methods like concurrency and parallelism can further improve data processing efficiency. Parallelism uses multi-core processors to accelerate calculations by breaking large workloads into smaller subtasks that can be done concurrently. Large datasets can be processed in a fraction of the time needed for sequential execution thanks to Python's multiprocessing package, which enables the parallel execution of functions. Contrarily, concurrency allows several processes to advance concurrently, especially for I/O-bound procedures. Python's asyncio package makes asynchronous programming possible, which can improve the efficiency of operations like data fetching and network queries.

A further essential component of designing effective code is memory management. Effective memory management prevents system resources from being depleted, which can cause lags or crashes, particularly when working with big datasets. Memory overhead can be significantly decreased using memory-efficient data structures and lazy loading, which loads data only when needed. Rather than putting a whole list into memory, Python's generators, for example, enable building iterators that yield items one at a time, saving memory.

Benchmarking and profiling techniques are crucial for locating bottlenecks and enhancing code performance. Profiling programs such as cProfile and line profiler provide comprehensive data on the time and memory used by different code segments. By examining these reports, data scientists can identify inefficient code parts and concentrate their optimization efforts where they will have the biggest impact. Finding the best method for a task is aided by benchmarking, which compares the effectiveness of various implementations.

Following software engineering best practices, such as modularity and reusability, is another aspect of writing efficient code. In addition to making the code easier to maintain and debug, breaking it down into smaller, reusable functions or modules encourages code reuse and eliminates redundancy. It is easier for other team members to comprehend and contribute to the codebase when clear and consistent coding methods are used, such as adhering to Python's PEP 8 style guide.

In order to preserve the dependability and maintainability of efficient code, testing and documentation are equally crucial. Clear descriptions of the functions and purposes of various code segments are provided by well documented code, which makes updates and alterations simpler. It is ensured that the code functions as intended and that modifications or optimizations do not generate new defects by writing unit tests and incorporating continuous testing procedures.

In summary, practical data science and analytics code requires algorithmic parallelism, optimization, vectorization, memory management, profiling, and adherence to recommended coding practices. By adhering to these criteria, data scientists can write code that is scalable, readable, maintainable and performs effectively. The foundation of any successful data science project is efficient code, which makes it possible to create reliable analytical models and extract valuable insights from massive datasets.

CHAPTER V

Data Visualization

Principles of Effective Visualization

A key component of data science and analytics is effective visualization, which acts as a potent medium for disseminating insights extracted from complex datasets. The fundamental tenets of this discipline are simplicity, relevance, clarity, and aesthetic appeal. The most important factor is clarity, which means that information must be represented through visualizations in a clear and intelligible way. In order to do this, it's important to apply visualization tools skillfully and avoid clutter that could obscure important ideas. Clarity is enhanced by simplicity, which promotes minimalist design. By eliminating unnecessary features, viewers may focus their attention on the most important information and quickly and intuitively comprehend the insights, empowering them in their data-understanding journey.

Another crucial aspect that becomes apparent is relevance, which requires that visualizations be customized to the unique requirements and goals of their target audience. This means having a thorough awareness of both the audience's tastes and expectations as well as the data that is already available. Visualizations gain impact and actionability when they are matched to the demands of the audience. Visualizations become even more engaging and understandable when they have an appealing aesthetic, making them more enticing and memorable. Careful design decisions about font, color scheme, and arrangement enhance the visual attractiveness of visualizations overall and have a significant impact on how viewers interpret the data, emphasizing the audience's integral role in the data interpretation process.

One of the most critical components of an effective visualization is scalability, which is the ability of a visualization to adjust to various data scales and contexts. Whether a scalable visualization is printed on a giant poster or seen on a small screen, it should always be understandable and informative. It means elements like aspect ratio, resolution, and detail level must be carefully considered. Scalability allows visualizations to remain accessible and versatile on various platforms and devices.

Another critical component of a successful visualization is interaction, which enables users to explore data dynamically and interactively discover insights. Users can change visual elements to obtain deeper insights, dive down into specific data points, and filter information based on criteria of interest while using interactive visualizations. Interactive visualizations enable people to actively engage with data and extract meaning on their terms, which can lead to more insightful and meaningful findings.

Effective visualization also heavily relies on storytelling, giving the data context and a narrative structure. Visualizations become more memorable and engaging when they frame data within an intriguing tale. This draws viewers in and helps them follow the story as it is being told. This entails developing a concise plot, arranging the visual components to support the narrative flow, and using strategies like annotations and highlighters to draw attention to important details.

Effective visualization necessitates ethical considerations, which dictate the representation and interpretation of data. The underlying data should be faithfully reflected in visualizations, and viewers should not be misled or distorted. This calls for openness in data collection, processing, and display and a dedication to moral behavior like protecting user privacy and guaranteeing data security. Visualizations preserve integrity and reliability by adhering to ethical principles and encouraging faith in their shared insights.

To sum up, the fundamentals of good visualization form the basis for producing powerful and perceptive visualizations in data science and analytics. Visualizations become more approachable, engaging, and practical by prioritizing simplicity, clarity, relevance, and aesthetic appeal. The usefulness of visualizations is further enhanced by scalability, interaction, storytelling, and ethical issues, allowing them to convey complicated findings engaging and reliably. To fully realize the potential of data-driven insights, one must become proficient in effective visualization, as data plays a significant role in decision-making across many sectors.

Tools and Techniques: Matplotlib, Seaborn, Tableau

In the rapidly developing field of data science and analytics, selecting the right tools and methods is essential to gaining valuable insights from large, complicated datasets. Three well-known tools stick out from the wide range of options: Matplotlib, Seaborn, and Tableau. One of the main components of the Python ecosystem, Matplotlib, provides a flexible and robust foundation for producing static, interactive, and publication-quality visuals. With its wide range of adaptable features and plotting functions, data scientists may create visual representations of data that clarify patterns, trends, and correlations. Based on Matplotlib, Seaborn offers a high-level interface for making visually appealing and educational statistical visualizations, substantially improving visualization capabilities. Seaborn is a vital tool for data scientists, allowing for quick data exploration and analysis thanks to its simple syntax and integrated support for intricate statistical visualizations.

Conversely, Tableau sets itself apart as a feature-rich data visualization tool that prioritizes usability and interactive exploration. A more comprehensive range of people, including decision-makers and business stakeholders, may create dynamic dashboards and visualizations using its simple drag-and-drop interface without coding. Tableau's powerful features go beyond simple charting to predictive modeling, advanced analytics, and global mapping. These features help users make data-driven decisions and gain deeper insights. Furthermore, Tableau's robust sharing and collaboration tools and connection with various data sources make it easier for enterprises to share information and execute efficient workflows.

Tableau excels at producing sophisticated, interactive presentations for a non-technical audience, whereas Matplotlib and Seaborn are superior in exploratory data analysis and statistical visualization. Each tool has its own advantages to meet the many demands and preferences of the data science and analytics community. Furthermore, combining these tools enables a comprehensive approach to data visualization: Tableau can be utilized for insights presentation and distribution to a broader audience, while Matplotlib and Seaborn may be used for in-depth research and visualization prototyping.

Each tool has a unique set of best practices, methods for maximizing effectiveness, and capabilities. A thorough understanding of the customization options and APIs offered by Matplotlib and Seaborn enables users to fine tune visualizations to satisfy individual requirements and aesthetic preferences. Methods like color mapping, data aggregation, and layering can improve the impact and clarity of visualizations while maintaining the simplicity, relevance, and scalability that are essential components of good visualization.

In the same way, Tableau users may use a vast array of features and functionalities to produce engaging and dynamic dashboards. Visual tales that are both interesting and educational can be made by utilizing strategies like storytelling through data, filter and parameter optimization, and dashboard design concepts. Additionally, Tableau's interface with sophisticated analytics programs like R and Python makes it possible to immediately incorporate statistical analysis and machine learning models into visualizations, which enhances the insights obtained from data.

In data science and analytics, Matplotlib, Seaborn, and Tableau are practical tools and methods for data visualization. Within the data science community, every tool caters to different needs and tastes, each bringing unique qualities. Data scientists can extract meaningful insights, promote informed decision-making throughout businesses, and realize the full potential of their data by utilizing the capabilities of these technologies and best practices and approaches. Maintaining competitiveness and optimizing the value of data-driven insights will require keeping up with developments in these tools and methodologies as the sector continues to change.

Creating Interactive Dashboards

As a dynamic and user-friendly interface for analyzing and sharing insights from large, complicated datasets, interactive dashboard creation is a high point in data science and analytics. An interactive dashboard is a central repository that unifies several data sources into a coherent and eye-catching representation. Users may interactively examine data, identify trends, and get real time actionable insights using these dashboards. Many processes involve making an interactive dashboard, from gathering and preparing data to designing and deploying the visualization.

The first step in the process is data acquisition, which involves gathering raw data from various sources, including databases, streaming services, APIs, and spreadsheets. This data is subsequently preprocessed and cleansed to guarantee quality and consistency, setting the stage for insightful analysis and visualization. After the data is ready, the following stage is to choose suitable visualization methods and create a user-friendly and visually appealing dashboard layout. Successfully communicating the insights found in the data involves selecting the appropriate chart kinds, colors, and typefaces.

User experience (UX) design, which focuses on developing a fluid and understandable interface that leads users through the data discovery process, is a crucial component of interactive dashboard design. This entails logically arranging the visualizations, offering simple navigation, and adding interactive features like drill-down capabilities, drop-down menus, and filters. Interactive dashboards prioritizing UX design concepts are more engaging and user-friendly, promoting deeper data exploration and interaction.

The core of interactive dashboards is interaction, allowing users to alter visuals and examine data from various angles dynamically. Users can filter and go further into particular subsets of data using interactive features like buttons, sliders, and checkboxes, revealing insights that could otherwise go unnoticed. In addition, tooltips and hover effects offer more context and details, making visualizations more straightforward and encouraging in depth research.

Performance optimization is another essential component of interactive dashboard design. It guarantees that dashboards stay scalable and responsive even while processing massive amounts of data. Optimizing dashboard load times entails refining data queries and calculations, caching frequently accessed data, and utilizing strategies like lazy loading. Regardless of the complexity or volume of the underlying data, interactive dashboards prioritize speed optimization to deliver a flawless user experience.

Security and data privacy are as important as design and performance factors when building interactive dashboards. This is especially true in workplace settings involving sensitive or proprietary data. Strong authentication, encryption, and access controls are needed to protect data from misuse or illegal access. Interactive dashboards provide users and stakeholders with confidence by upholding stringent security procedures that preserve the confidentiality and integrity of the data they carry.

The interactive dashboard's deployment and distribution to end users constitute the last phase after it has been planned and produced. Numerous platforms, including specialized dashboard platforms, mobile applications, and web browsers, can accomplish this. Regular maintenance and upgrades are also necessary to keep the dashboard current and relevant in the face of shifting data and business needs. Organizations can get the most out of their interactive dashboards and promote data-driven decision-making throughout the company by iteratively improving the dashboard in response to user feedback and changing data patterns.

Building interactive dashboards is a complex process that includes gathering and preparing data and designing visualizations, user experiences, interactivity, performance optimization, security, and deployment. By skillfully combining these components, data scientists and analysts may create immersive and captivating experiences that enable people to explore data, find insights, and make well-informed decisions. Interactive dashboards will remain essential in democratizing data access and developing a culture of data-driven decision-making as businesses depend increasingly on data to inform strategic objectives and achieve a competitive edge.

CHAPTER VI

Machine Learning Basics

Supervised vs. Unsupervised Learning

Supervised and unsupervised learning are two essential data science and analytics methods for drawing conclusions and patterns from data. In supervised learning, a model is trained using labeled data, with each observation correlated with a relevant goal variable or outcome. Learning a mapping from input attributes to output labels is the aim of supervised learning, which enables the model to make predictions on new, unseen data. Classification and regression are common supervised learning problems that aim to predict continuous numerical values and discrete labels given input data, respectively.

On the other hand, unsupervised learning uses unlabeled data and aims to find underlying structures or patterns in the data without direct supervision or instruction. Unlike supervised learning, unsupervised learning tasks do not require labeled data, making them especially useful for exploratory data analysis and revealing previously undiscovered insights. Typical unsupervised learning methods include dimensionality reduction, which aims to minimize the number of features in the data while maintaining its fundamental properties, and clustering, which groups data points into clusters based on proximity or similarity.

Depending on the type of data and the particular goals of the study, each approach has a unique combination of benefits and drawbacks. For example, supervised learning performs best when the job includes making predictions or classifying new observations, and labeled data is easily accessible. Using the wealth of information found in labeled data, supervised learning models can identify intricate linkages and patterns that result in precise and trustworthy predictions. Supervised learning, however, is highly dependent on the representativeness and quality of the labeled data, which can be difficult or expensive to obtain, particularly in fields where manual annotation or expert knowledge is needed for labeling.

However, unsupervised learning provides a more adaptable and exploratory method of analyzing data, enabling the identification of new structures and patterns without the requirement for labeled data. Natural groups or clusters within the data can be found using unsupervised learning approaches like clustering, showing underlying commonalities or relationships that would not be obvious from the raw data alone. Additionally, unsupervised learning is beneficial for anomaly detection, which involves finding uncommon or infrequent occurrences in a dataset. Unsupervised learning models can help find abnormalities or outliers that may reveal fraud, errors, or other strange behavior by identifying departures from the norm, which might signal potential anomalies for further study.

Despite their distinctions, supervised and unsupervised learning frequently work well together in practical data analysis contexts and are not mutually exclusive. For instance, semi-supervised learning leverages a small pool of labeled data and a larger pool of unlabeled data to incorporate both supervised and unsupervised learning aspects. With the help of this hybrid strategy, the required manual labeling can be significantly reduced, and the insights obtained by unsupervised learning techniques can still be beneficial.

In addition, there is another paradigm in machine learning that is distinct from supervised and unsupervised learning: reinforcement learning. Through trial and error, an agent learns how to interact with its environment through reinforcement learning. It receives feedback through rewards or penalties depending on what it does. Reward sequences, like those in gaming, robotics, and autonomous vehicles, are ideal for reinforcement learning because the agent learns to optimize its behavior over time to maximize cumulative rewards.

To sum up, there are two fundamental approaches to data science and analytics: supervised and unsupervised learning, each with advantages and uses. Supervised learning performs exceptionally well when there is a large amount of labeled data, including making predictions or classifying fresh observations. Conversely, unsupervised learning provides a more exploratory method of data analysis, making it possible to find underlying structures and patterns in unlabeled data. Data scientists and analysts can select the most suitable strategies to extract insights and facilitate well-informed decision-making across many domains by comprehending the advantages and disadvantages of each approach.

Key Algorithms: Linear Regression, Decision Trees, Clustering

Key algorithms like Linear Regression, Decision Trees, and Clustering are essential for gaining insights, generating predictions, and identifying patterns in significant, complicated data science and analytics datasets. One of the fundamental methods in supervised learning is linear regression, which is especially useful for problems that require predicting a continuous numerical result variable from one or more input data. Analysts can generate predictions and comprehend the underlying relationships between variables by using Linear Regression, which fits a linear model to the data and estimates the relationship between the independent and dependent variables. Linear regression is a flexible tool for various predictive modeling activities, from price and trend analysis to sales forecasting and risk assessment. Its simplicity, interpretability, and ease of application contribute to its versatility.

Decision trees, on the other hand, provide a non parametric method of supervised learning that can work with both numerical and categorical data. Based on the values of the input features, decision trees divide the feature space into hierarchical binary splits, which eventually result in a tree-like structure where each leaf node represents a predicted result or class label. Decision Trees are a popular tool for tasks where interpretability is crucial because of their transparent and intuitive decision making process. Additionally, Decision Trees are simple to understand and display, which gives analysts a better understanding of the decision-making process and helps them pinpoint critical variables that influence forecasts. Decision trees are easy to use, but they can perform poorly in generalizing new data due to overfitting, especially when dealing with complicated datasets. To counteract this problem, ensemble methods like Random Forests and Gradient Boosting Machines combine several decision trees to increase the precision and resilience of their predictions.

Another essential unsupervised learning algorithm is clustering, which divides data points into discrete groups or clusters according to proximity or similarity. In contrast to supervised learning, clustering relies just on the properties of the data and doesn't need labeled input. K means, Hierarchical Clustering, and DBSCAN are popular clustering methods; each has advantages and disadvantages. For instance, K-means divides data points into K clusters by updating cluster centroids iteratively to reduce the sum of squared distances inside a cluster. In contrast, hierarchical clustering creates a hierarchy of clusters by repeatedly combining or dividing clusters according to their pairwise distances. Density-based clustering algorithm DBSCAN clusters closely spaced data points together and labels noise in the case of outliers. Applications for clustering algorithms can be found in many different fields, including recommendation systems, anomaly detection, picture segmentation, and consumer segmentation.

Although Clustering, Decision Trees, and Linear Regression are independent algorithms with separate goals and approaches, they are all based on similar ideas and strategies that make them work well together. For instance, feature engineering is essential in getting ready data for analysis since it finds, modifies, and extracts pertinent features that record significant information. The proper formatting and standardization of input data for various algorithms is ensured by normalization, scaling, and encoding categorical variables. Furthermore, evaluating and validating predictive models are crucial processes in determining how well they work and how well they can generalize. Metrics that quantify model performance and aid in model selection and improvement include Mean Squared Error (MSE), Accuracy, Precision, Recall, and Silhouette Score.

To sum up, three important algorithms in data science and analytics are clustering, decision trees, and linear regression. Each has a unique set of uses and capabilities. In a supervised learning environment, linear regression can predict outcomes and determine how variables relate. Decision trees offer an understandable and visible framework for predictive modeling, whereas clustering provides information about the underlying structure of unlabeled data. By comprehending the underlying ideas and approaches, data scientists and analysts can effectively utilize these algorithms to extract insights, generate predictions, and facilitate data-driven decision making in various areas.

Model Evaluation and Validation

In data science and analytics, model evaluation and validation are essential components that offer the capacity to gauge the efficacy of prediction models in practical settings and to evaluate their performance and dependability. Fundamentally, model assessment compares a model's predictions to observed results or known ground truth values, whereas model validation evaluates the model's capacity to generalize to new data. These procedures are essential for selecting the suitable model, fine-tuning hyperparameters, and locating potential sources of variance or bias that could compromise the model's performance.

Accuracy, which quantifies the percentage of correctly identified cases among all instances, is one of the primary metrics used to assess the model. Even though accuracy offers a simple way to gauge the model's overall performance, it's not necessarily the best indicator, especially when there's a class gap or asymmetric costs. Other metrics that account for the trade-offs between true positives, false positives, true negatives, and false negatives, such as precision, recall, F1 score, and area under the receiver operating characteristic curve (AUC-

ROC), provide more sophisticated performance assessments in these situations.

Cross-validation is a popular method for validating models, which is especially useful when the dataset is small, or the data distribution is not uniform. In cross validation, the dataset is divided into several folds or subsets, and the model is trained on a portion of the data. At the same time, its performance is assessed on the remaining data. This process is done several times to get an overall estimate of the model's performance, using each fold as a training and validation set. The results are averaged. Cross-validation reduces the danger of overfitting by giving a more reliable assessment of the model's performance on unobserved data.

Validation and learning curves, which show how model performance changes with changes in model complexity, dataset size, and other hyperparameters, are two more popular methods for evaluating models. By plotting model performance indicators like accuracy or error rate as a function of a specific hyperparameter, validation curves help analysts determine the ideal value that will optimize the model's performance. In contrast, learning curves show how model performance relates to dataset size, which makes it easier to determine if the model would benefit from more data or has reached a performance plateau.

Additionally, evaluating the model's stability and robustness across various datasets and settings is critical to model evaluation and validation. Through the random selection of subsets of the data or the introduction of random perturbations to the data during training, techniques like bootstrap resampling and Monte Carlo cross-validation provide estimates of model variability. Analysts can confirm the model's generalizability to new data and obtain insights into its stability and reliability under varying situations by assessing model performance across numerous iterations or variations of the dataset.

In addition, techniques for identifying and addressing sources of bias, variation, and overfitting that could impair model performance are included in model evaluation. The variance shows how sensitive the model is to changes in the training data, whereas bias relates to systematic errors or inaccuracies in the predictions made by the model. Poor generalization performance on unknown data is caused by overfitting, which happens when the model learns to capture noise or unimportant patterns in the training set. Techniques like regularization, feature selection, and ensemble approaches to solve these problems by promoting simpler models, reducing model complexity, and aggregating numerous models to improve predictive performance.

Ethical issues are also very important when evaluating and validating models, especially in fields where predictive models are used to make decisions that significantly influence people or society as a whole. Analysts must guarantee that models are equitable, lucid, and responsible and that they do not reinforce or intensify any preexisting biases within the data. Methods that help reduce bias and increase transparency include model explainability and fairness-aware machine learning, which reveal how models make decisions and what influences their predictions.

To sum up, model validation and assessment are essential in creating and applying predictive models in data science and analytics. Analysts can choose the best model, adjust hyperparameters, and pinpoint probable sources of bias or variance by methodically evaluating the model's robustness, performance, and dependability. Furthermore, analysts can guarantee that prediction models are reliable and consistent with societal goals by upholding moral standards and encouraging openness and responsibility. To fully utilize predictive analytics and have a good social impact, one must become proficient in assessing and validating models since data is becoming increasingly important in decision-making across a range of sectors.

CHAPTER VII

Advanced Machine Learning

Deep Learning and Neural Networks

Data science and analytics have undergone a paradigm shift thanks to deep learning and neural networks, which have never been able to predict intricate correlations and patterns in large datasets. The neural network, a computer model based on the composition and operation of the human brain, is the fundamental component of deep learning. Artificial neurons are arranged in interconnected layers to form neural networks, and each layer processes incoming data through several mathematical operations to produce meaningful representations. Neural networks can learn hierarchical representations of data by stacking layers of neurons. This allows the networks to identify complex patterns and connections that could be challenging to identify using conventional machine learning methods.

One of its main advantages is deep learning's capacity to autonomously extract feature representations from unprocessed data, doing away with the requirement for human feature engineering. Handcrafted features are often necessary for traditional machine learning algorithms to extract pertinent data information. On the other hand, deep learning models can adapt to a wide range of tasks and domains because they can learn abstract and hierarchical representations of data straight from raw inputs. Because of the complexity and variety of the data, human feature engineering could be more practical in domains like speech recognition, computer vision, and natural language processing. This capacity has revolutionized these fields.

Convolutional Neural Networks (CNNs) are one of the most widely used deep learning architectures, especially in computer vision. Using layers of convolutional filters to extract local patterns and characteristics from the input image, CNNs are specifically made to handle spatially structured data, like images. CNNs can learn to identify objects, sceneries, and textures inside images by gradually merging low-level information into higher-level representations. This allows CNNs to perform state-of the-art tasks like object identification, image segmentation, and image classification.

Neural networks that are particularly good at modeling sequential data, like speech, text, and time-series data, are called recurrent neural networks (RNNs). RNNs preserve internal state, which enables them to capture temporal dependencies and context over time, in contrast to feedforward neural networks, which process input data in a single forward pass. This makes RNNs ideal for applications where deciphering the sequential structure of the data is crucial to producing precise predictions, like sentiment analysis, machine translation, and language modeling.

Moreover, deep learning has prompted the creation of increasingly complex structures and methodologies, like Generative Adversarial Networks (GANs) and Long Short Term Memory (LSTM) networks. A type of RNN called LSTM networks uses gating methods to control the information flow over time to solve the vanishing gradient issue. Because of this, LSTM networks may effectively handle tasks like speech recognition, machine translation, and time-series forecasting by capturing long-range dependencies and context in sequential data.

Conversely, GANs belong to a class of generative models that may produce new data samples based on a given distribution. The generator and the discriminator, the two neural networks that make up a GAN, are trained against each other to produce realistic samples and distinguish between created and actual data, respectively. Generative Adversarial Networks (GANs) can produce diverse and high-quality samples in several domains, including text, audio, and images, by iteratively refining the discriminator and generator networks. With applications ranging from digital art and entertainment to drug research and synthetic data synthesis, this has led to achievements in domains including image generation, style transfer, and data augmentation.

Deep learning models are compelling but have scalability, interpretability, and generalization drawbacks. Large volumes of labeled data and computer power are generally needed for deep neural networks to train efficiently, which limits their applicability to situations with limited resources or smaller businesses. Furthermore, deep learning models' complexity and opacity might make them difficult to understand and trust, especially in high-stakes situations where accountability and openness are crucial. Methods including adversarial robustness, uncertainty estimation, and model explainability are being actively studied to address these issues and improve the dependability and credibility of deep learning models.

To sum up, deep learning and neural networks are revolutionizing data science and analytics by making it possible to model intricate correlations and patterns in big datasets. Deep learning has fundamentally changed our capacity to study, comprehend, and produce data in various disciplines, from computer vision and natural language processing to speech recognition and generative modeling applications. Data scientists and analysts may drive innovation, uncover new insights, and make well informed decisions that benefit society by utilizing deep learning. But to fully use deep learning, scalability, interpretability, and generalization issues must be resolved. Additionally, ethical issues and societal norms must be respected when creating and applying deep learning models.

Natural Language Processing (NLP)

At the forefront of data science and analytics is natural language processing, or NLP, which provides: Effective methods for gaining insights. Deciphering human language. Facilitating communication between computers and people. Text classification, sentiment analysis, named entity identification, machine translation, question answering, and text generation are just a few of the many activities and applications that fall under the broad umbrella of natural language processing (NLP). NLP uses machine learning, deep learning, and computational linguistics to give computers the ability to comprehend and interpret human language in ways previously thought possible for humans.

Classifying text documents into predetermined categories or labels according to their content is one of the fundamental tasks of natural language processing (NLP). Applications for text classification can be found in many fields, including document categorization, sentiment analysis, topic modeling, and spam detection. Text classification is a common application for machine learning algorithms like Support Vector Machines (SVM), Naive Bayes, and deep learning models like Convolutional Neural Networks (CNNs) and Recurrent Neural Networks (RNNs). These models allow computers to automatically and accurately assign labels to text documents.

Determining the attitude or opinion communicated in a text using sentiment analysis is another significant use of natural language processing (NLP). Applications for sentiment analysis include market research, customer feedback analysis, brand reputation management, and social media monitoring. Organizations can discover new patterns, learn about customer perspectives, and make well-informed decisions to enhance their offerings by studying the sentiment of text data. To achieve state-of-the-art performance on sentiment classification tasks, supervised learning approaches, including Logistic Regression, Support Vector Machines, and deep learning models like Transformers and Long Short-Term Memory (LSTM) networks, are frequently employed for sentiment analysis tasks.

Another significant NLP problem is named entity recognition (NER), which is concerned with recognizing and classifying entities such as names of individuals, groups, places, dates, and other particular kinds of information stated in the text. Applications for NER include entity linkage, information extraction, document summarization, and question-answering systems. For NER tasks, machine learning models like Conditional Random Fields (CRF), Hidden Markov Models (HMM), and deep learning models like Transformer-based architectures and Bidirectional Long Short-Term Memory (BiLSTM) networks are frequently used. These models allow computers to recognize and extract relevant entities from text data automatically. Machine translation is one of the most challenging and significant uses of natural language processing (NLP) when translating text between languages.

Machine translation systems use neural machine translation, statistical machine translation, and transformer-based architectures to provide precise and natural-sounding translations across various languages. Through these platforms, people may now communicate with one another, obtain information, and conduct commerce across linguistic barriers, revolutionizing cross-cultural communication. Well-known machine translation systems include Microsoft Translator, Google Translate, and OpenAI's GPT-based models, which have demonstrated impressive results across various language pairs and areas.

Another area of NLP research is question answering, which aims to create systems that can comprehend and react to user-posed natural language queries. Question answering systems use strategies including knowledge representation, language understanding, and information retrieval to provide precise and pertinent responses to user inquiries. These systems are used in information retrieval systems, chatbots for customer service, and virtual assistants to help users acquire information and do activities more quickly. A combination of natural language processing (NLP) methods and machine learning algorithms are used by IBM Watson, Amazon Alexa, and Apple's Siri, among other question-answering systems, to comprehend and react to customer inquiries.

In summary, Natural Language Processing (NLP) is a topic that is revolutionizing data science and analytics by allowing computers to comprehend, analyze, and produce human language in ways that were previously believed to be human only. NLP offers various applications and chances for innovation across multiple disciplines, from named entity recognition, machine translation, and question answering to text categorization and sentiment analysis. Organizations may improve decision-making procedures, extract insightful information from text data, and improve how people interact with computers and information by utilizing NLP. However, issues with ambiguity, cultural subtleties, and language variety must be resolved to utilize NLP fully. Additionally, NLP systems must be developed and implemented with ethical and privacy concerns in mind.

Reinforcement Learning

A potent data science and analytics paradigm is reinforcement learning (RL), which provides a framework for teaching agents to make sequential decisions in dynamic contexts. Fundamentally, reinforcement learning (RL) draws inspiration from the ideas of behavioral psychology, in which agents experiment with their surroundings to maximize cumulative rewards. In contrast to labeled or unlabeled data-based supervised and unsupervised learning, reinforcement learning (RL) works in an interactive environment where agents learn from the results of their decisions and receive feedback in the form of rewards or penalties. Over the years, the agent's behavior is guided by this input, which helps it learn the best ways to accomplish its objectives in challenging and unpredictable circumstances.

The Markov Decision Process (MDP) is fundamental in reinforcement learning (RL). It represents the RL problem as a tuple with states, actions, transition probabilities, rewards, and a discount factor. Learning a policy, or a mapping from states to actions, that maximizes the predicted cumulative reward over time is the aim of a reinforcement learning agent. Through an iterative process called the reinforcement learning loop, the agent gains experience optimizing its policy by interacting with the environment, observing states, acting, and receiving rewards.

In data science and analytics, reinforcement learning (RL) has many uses across industries, including robotics, autonomous systems, gaming, finance, healthcare, and recommendation systems. Robotics uses reinforcement learning (RL) to teach agents sophisticated motor skills and control policies through interactions with their surroundings. This allows the agents to adapt to changing situations and carry out tasks, including navigation, manipulation, and locomotion. Robotics (RL) is used in autonomous systems to teach cars, drones, and other autonomous agents to make decisions like target tracking, obstacle avoidance, and route planning. In finance, RL algorithms can manage portfolios, hedge against risk, and optimize trading tactics in volatile and dynamic markets. Personalized treatment planning, medication development, and medical imaging analysis are just a few healthcare-related applications where RL can improve efficiency and effectiveness. Personalized and adaptive content suggestions, user engagement optimization, and dynamic pricing strategies are made possible by reinforcement learning (RL) in recommendation systems, which improve user experience and drive business outcomes in online platforms.

The exploration-exploitation trade-off, in which agents must balance utilizing existing actions and situations to maximize short-term rewards and exploring new actions and conditions to uncover optimal methods, is one of the main issues in reinforcement learning. To solve this trade off, strategies like Upper Confidence Bound (UCB) exploration, \-greedy exploration, and softmax exploration are frequently employed, which promote exploration while still taking advantage of the most well known actions. The curse of dimensionality, which occurs when the number of dimensions increases exponentially and makes state and action space complexity impossible to learn efficiently and accurately, is another problem in reinforcement learning. The curse of dimensionality is lessened by approximating value functions and policies in high-dimensional environments using strategies like function approximation, value iteration, and Monte Carlo approaches.

Furthermore, the application of deep neural networks to estimate value functions, policies, and action-value functions in high-dimensional state and action spaces has made deep reinforcement learning (DRL) a potent method for reinforcement learning. Several well-known DRL methods, including Deep Q-Learning (DQN), Deep Deterministic Policy Gradient (DDPG), Proximal Policy Optimization (PPO), and Trust Region Policy Optimization (TRPO), achieve state-of-the-art performance in a variety of RL problems. With the ability for agents to learn complicated behaviors and decision-making policies directly from raw sensory inputs like photos, videos, and sensor data, DRL has transformed sectors like gaming, robotics, and autonomous systems.

CHAPTER VIII

Business Analytics

Understanding Business Needs

To guarantee that the insights and solutions produced by data experts suit the strategic objectives and operational demands of the company, an understanding of business needs is a fundamental component of data science and analytics. Achieving measurable business outcomes and creating value requires this alignment. The first step in the process is to fully understand the business context, including the industry, market dynamics, competitive environment, and particular difficulties the company faces. Data scientists can comprehensively understand the needs and priorities of the company by interacting with stakeholders from many departments.

Finding the organization's main aims and objectives is the initial step towards comprehending business needs. These can include raising sales, cutting expenses, raising customer satisfaction, boosting operational effectiveness, and encouraging innovation. Data scientists should have conversations with business executives to understand these goals and how data-driven insights might help them. This calls on excellent communication skills and technical expertise to bridge the gap between technical and non-technical stakeholders. Data scientists can then use this information to translate business goals into precise, quantifiable, and valuable data science initiatives.

The next stage is to determine the metrics and key performance indicators (KPIs) that will be used to gauge success after the objectives are understood. Different company domains have different KPIs. For instance, in marketing, client acquisition costs, lifetime values, and conversion rates may be considered; in operations, supply chain efficiency, production costs, and cycle durations may be the critical focus areas. Data scientists must comprehend these metrics to create models and analyses offering pertinent insights. By working with stakeholders to establish these KPIs, data science initiatives are guaranteed to align with business priorities.

The process of comprehending company needs requires careful consideration of both data preparation and collecting. The pertinent internal and external data sources that can offer the necessary information for analysis must be located by data scientists. Working closely with the IT and data management teams is essential to guarantee the accessibility, quality, and availability of data. Data preparation involves combining, cleaning, and manipulating data from multiple sources to build a coherent dataset fit for analysis. Although time consuming, this step is crucial to guaranteeing the precision and dependability of the insights produced.

After the data is produced, data scientists use various analytical methods to find links, patterns, and trends that can help guide business choices. Businesses may comprehend historical performance and pinpoint areas for development using descriptive analytics, which offers a historical perspective of the data. To understand the underlying reasons for noticed patterns and trends, diagnostic analytics digs deeper. Businesses can foresee changes and take proactive measures using predictive analytics, which uses statistical and machine learning models to estimate future results. Prescriptive analytics takes one step further by offering recommendations for particular courses of action predicated on data-driven insights. Data scientists can offer thorough insights that meet the needs of the business by combining various methods.

Effective insight communication is a critical component of knowing business demands. Data scientists need to communicate their findings to non-technical stakeholders clearly, succinctly, and engagingly. This includes producing reports, dashboards, and visualizations highlighting essential conclusions and suggestions. Good communication guarantees that all involved can quickly comprehend the data's consequences and use the insights to make well-informed decisions. Narrative approaches can be beneficial since they help place the data in the context of the larger corporate story.

Awareness of business demands necessitates a thorough understanding of the sector and domain in which the company operates, as well as technical and analytical abilities. Data scientists are better equipped to ask pertinent questions, interpret data correctly, and offer insightful analysis when they possess domain knowledge. For instance, developing successful data science solutions in the healthcare sector requires a thorough understanding of clinical workflows, patient care procedures, and regulatory constraints. Similarly, in the financial industry, creating models that offer valuable insights requires a comprehensive understanding of market patterns, risk management, and regulatory compliance.

Comprehending the ethical and legal ramifications of data science initiatives is crucial to comprehending commercial requirements. Data scientists must follow the laws and regulations that apply to their analysis and recommendations—such as those about data privacy and protection—. This calls for keeping up with regulatory requirements and working with legal and compliance teams to guarantee that data science procedures are morally sound. Making sure data science initiatives don't unintentionally promote bias or discrimination and that they benefit both the company and society is another aspect of ethical issues.

To sum up, a key component of data science and analytics is comprehending business demands, guaranteeing that data-driven insights align with organizational objectives. Data scientists may create value and facilitate well informed decision-making through stakeholder engagement, key objective, and KPI identification, relevant data collection and preparation, advanced analytical techniques, and effective insight communication. It also takes a thorough grasp of the field, industry, and legal and ethical issues to build moral and successful data science solutions. Data scientists may fully utilize data to solve business problems and accomplish strategic goals using an all-inclusive strategy.

Key Performance Indicators (KPIs)

For data science and analytics, Key Performance Indicators (KPIs) are essential for gauging the overall impact, efficacy, and efficiency of data-driven projects inside a company. Strong KPIs highlighting the effectiveness and worth of data science and analytics initiatives are crucial, as data plays a more significant role in strategic decision-making. These KPIs support progress monitoring, problem identification, and alignment with organizational goals.

Predictive model accuracy is a key performance indicator (KPI) in data science and analytics. The degree to which a model's predictions agree with the actual results is called its accuracy. A high accuracy rate suggests that the model is trustworthy and can be used to make judgments. But more than precision on its own is required. Other metrics offer a more comprehensive view of a model's performance, including precision, recall, and F1-score, especially in imbalanced datasets where one class may predominate. By reducing false positives and negatives, these metrics aid in assessing the model's accuracy in identifying true positives and negatives.

Another important KPI is the return on investment (ROI), which measures the financial gains made from data science and analytics initiatives compared to their expenses. Evaluating the economic benefits of better decision-making, cost reductions, or revenue generation attributable to data-driven insights is calculating return on investment. A positive return on investment (ROI) signifies that the analytics endeavors yield benefits and enhance the company's financial performance. This measure is especially crucial for proving to stakeholders the actual returns on these endeavors and defending additional expenditures in data science capabilities.

One KPI that is essential to pay attention to is data quality. High-quality underlying data is critical to the success of data science efforts. KPIs for data quality include measurements of the data's timeliness, accuracy, consistency, and completeness. High-quality data guarantees the reliability and actionability of the insights produced. Organizations frequently use data quality indices or scores to assess and enhance their data quality continuously. This proactive strategy aids in averting data problems that can jeopardize the validity of analytics initiatives.

KPIs measuring customer engagement and satisfaction are extremely important, especially for analytics initiatives that enhance the customer experience. Numerous techniques can be used to calculate these KPIs, including customer satisfaction surveys, net promoter scores (NPS), and customer retention rates. By looking at these measures, organizations can assess how their data driven strategies affect customer satisfaction and loyalty. Enhancements in these domains frequently result in higher income and a more significant portion of the market, underscoring the need to match analytics initiatives with customer-focused objectives.

KPIs are also essential for operational efficiency. This can be quantified in data science and analytics using measures like data processing speed, model development and deployment time, and task automation. Efficiency KPIs give firms a better understanding of how well they are using their analytics and data resources. Quicker deployment and processing times point to an analytics department that is more flexible and agile, able to quickly adjust to shifting business requirements.

Additional KPIs that illuminate the usefulness and significance of analytics solutions include user adoption and engagement with analytics tools and platforms. Metrics that show how widely analytics tools are used within the company include the number of active users, how often they are used, and how diverse the user base is across departments. Low adoption rates could indicate the need for further assistance, training, or tool enhancement, whereas high adoption rates indicate that the tools are valuable and easy to use.

In the age of complicated machine learning models, know-how metrics such as model interpretability and transparency are becoming increasingly crucial. Making sure that models are interpretable helps stakeholders understand the decision-making process, which fosters trust and facilitates regulatory compliance. The percentage of models that have undergone interpretability evaluations, the number of stakeholders who have received model interpretation training, and the frequency of interpretability audits are key performance indicators (KPIs) in this domain.

Finally, research and development (R&D)-related KPIs, such as the number of new models created, the uptake of cutting-edge technologies, and the frequency of updates to current models, can be used to monitor innovation and ongoing progress in data science and analytics. These KPIs show how dedicated a company is to keeping at the forefront of data science and analytics, ensuring they are constantly enhancing their skills and taking advantage of the most recent developments in the industry.

To sum up, data science and analytics KPIs are crucial for gauging the success, economy, and influence of data based projects. Organizations may ensure that their data science initiatives align with business objectives and provide real value by monitoring KPIs, including model accuracy, ROI, data quality, customer happiness, operational efficiency, user adoption, model interpretability, and innovation. These KPIs offer a thorough framework for evaluating results, pinpointing areas needing development, and promoting ongoing improvement in data science and analytics procedures.

Predictive and Prescriptive Analytics

Predictive and prescriptive analytics are two innovative methods in data science and analytics that significantly improve decision-making across various businesses. These methods convert raw data into actionable insights that propel strategic objectives using past data and advanced algorithms to estimate future results and suggest the best action.

The main goal of predictive analytics is to project future events using past data. It uses various statistical methods, machine learning algorithms, and data mining strategies to find patterns and trends. Predicting what is likely to happen in a given situation is the core purpose of predictive analytics. Predictive analytics, for example, can estimate stock prices or credit risks in the finance industry by examining historical financial data. It can forecast patient outcomes and the chance of disease outbreaks in the healthcare industry, allowing for preventative interventions. Predictive analytics is used by retail organizations to improve consumer segmentation for focused marketing efforts, forecast demand, and optimize inventory levels.

Data collection, the first step in predictive analytics, is obtaining pertinent historical data from various sources. After that, this data is cleaned and preprocessed to deal with inconsistent data, outliers, and missing values. Following feature engineering and selection, essential variables are found and modified to fit the modeling procedure better. Depending on the data type and prediction problem, the next step is choosing suitable predictive models, such as ensemble approaches, decision trees, neural networks, and regression analysis. Historical data is used for training and validation to guarantee the accuracy and dependability of these models. After being verified, they are used to forecast fresh data, offering insightful information that helps in decision-making.

Conversely, prescriptive analytics suggests particular actions that can affect future outcomes in addition to forecasting them. It blends optimization strategies, business rules, and prediction models to recommend the optimum course of action. Prescriptive analytics aims not only to anticipate future events but also to elucidate the reasons behind their likelihood and provide strategies for capitalizing on them. This method works exceptionally well in complicated decision-making because it considers various elements and possible outcomes. Prescriptive analytics suggest ideal inventory levels, sourcing tactics, and shipping schedules in supply chain management to save money and increase efficiency. It can provide tailored pricing and marketing promotion plans with the best return on investment.

Prescriptive analytics can guide treatment strategies and resource allocation in the healthcare industry to enhance patient outcomes and operational effectiveness. Preprocessing and data collecting are the first steps in deploying prescriptive analytics, comparable to predictive analytics. Still, it goes further by adding simulation methods and optimization models. These models assess different situations and possible results while accounting for limitations and goals unique to the business environment. To determine the optimal course of action, methods including Monte Carlo simulations, integer programming, and linear programming are frequently employed. Furthermore, prescriptive analytics often interfaces with decision-support platforms to deliver recommendations in real-time and streamline the decision-making process.

Prescriptive and predictive analytics work very well together. Prescriptive analytics delivers the direction required to successfully traverse these events, while predictive analytics provides the necessary foresight to comprehend possible future scenarios. When combined, they give businesses the ability to not only foresee changes but also to adjust and react early. This integration may result from significant competitive advantages, such as increased profitability, better customer satisfaction, and operational efficiency.

Prescriptive and predictive analytics have several applications in a variety of industries. They improve investing methods, fraud detection, and risk management in the financial sector. Inventory control, targeted marketing, and optimal pricing are advantageous to retailers. Data-driven insights help healthcare providers control costs and improve patient outcomes. The manufacturing sector uses these analytics to optimize supply chain dynamics, forecast equipment failures, and streamline production operations. Public sectors, including government and education, use prescription, ve, and predictive analytics to formulate policies, allocate resources, and enhance public services.

However, overcoming several obstacles is necessary for applying prescriptive and predictive analytics practically. Data availability and quality are vital because adequate or accurate data might produce untrustworthy forecasts and recommendations. It is also crucial to ensure data security and privacy, especially in sensitive data industries. Adoption may also be hampered by model complexity and the requirement for specialist knowledge. Organizations need to make training and development investments for their staff to use these cutting-edge analytics technologies to their full potential.

In summary, the ultimate in data science capabilities are represented by predictive and prescriptive analytics, which enable businesses to predict the future and take well-informed decisions that lead to success. These approaches offer a thorough framework for proactive and strategic decision-making using historical data, cutting-edge algorithms, and optimization strategies. Prescriptive and prescriptive analytics integration will be more and more necessary as data volume and significance increase. This will help firms prosper in a competitive and ever- changing environment.

CHAPTER IX

Healthcare Analytics

Electronic Health Records (EHR) Analysis

Electronic Health Records (EHRs) have completely changed the healthcare sector through the digitization of patient data, enabling better patient care, more operational efficiency, and thorough data analysis. Leveraging the massive volumes of data in EHRs to extract insightful knowledge that can improve clinical decision-making, optimize healthcare delivery, and spur medical research, EHR analysis for data science and analytics has developed as a critical field.

A vast array of patient data is included in electronic health records (EHRs), such as demographics, medical histories, diagnoses, prescriptions, treatment plans, dates of immunizations, allergies, radiological pictures, and laboratory test results. When properly examined, this abundance of data might reveal patterns and trends that influence different facets of healthcare. Improving patient outcomes is one of the primary uses of EHR analysis. Healthcare professionals can discover risk factors and early warning indications of diseases by reviewing previous patient interventions. data, Predictive which enables prompt analytics models can significantly improve patient prognoses to forecast health trajectories and recommend early treatments or preventive measures.

Additionally, EHR analysis supports personalized medicine, a rapidly developing discipline that customizes medical care to each patient's unique traits. Data science methods can evaluate genetic and conventional medical data to find the best treatments for particular patient subgroups. For example, cancer treatment might be enhanced by identifying individuals who are more likely to respond to a specific medication of chemotherapy based on their genetic composition and previous responses recorded in their electronic health records. This customized strategy lowers side effects and medical expenses while improving treatment efficacy.

Through EHR analysis, operational efficiency inside healthcare facilities can also significantly increase. Patient wait times can be shortened, administrative procedures can be streamlined, and resource allocation can be optimized via data analytics. Hospitals can more efficiently allocate staff and resources by forecasting peak times by analyzing patient flow data. EHR analysis also can spot inefficiencies in clinical workflows, which can result in the adoption of more cost- and time-effective procedures.

Additionally, public health gains a great deal from EHR studies. EHR data that has been aggregated and anonymized can shed light on disease outbreaks, population health patterns, and the efficacy of public health initiatives. Public health officials must use this information to make well-informed decisions about vaccination campaigns, resource distribution, and epidemic response. For example, EHR data was critical in monitoring infection rates, identifying high-risk individuals, and assessing the efficacy of vaccines and therapies during the COVID-19 pandemic.

In addition, EHR analysis is a potent instrument in medicine. The extensive information that EHRs make available to researchers can be used to validate clinical trial outcomes and epidemiological studies and identify possible novel therapeutic targets. Access to long-term data from various populations improves the validity of study results and hastens the advancement of new medical understanding. Machine learning and artificial intelligence (AI) approaches are beneficial because they can go through large datasets and find relationships and patterns that might take time.

The examination of EHR data is challenging, though. Because medical data is sensitive, ensuring data privacy and security is critical. In the US, laws like the Health Insurance Portability and Accountability Act (HIPAA) require tight restrictions over who can access and use patient data. Healthcare institutions must follow these standards. Techniques for de-identification and anonymization are frequently used to safeguard patient privacy while allowing for critical data analysis.

Data quality is still another essential concern. Because of human mistakes or variations in data input procedures between institutions, electronic health records (EHRs) may have errors, insufficient information, and inconsistencies. Standardization and data cleaning are crucial phases in the analytical process that guarantee the conclusions' validity. Another significant issue is interoperability across various EHR systems since disparate formats and standards can make data integration and sharing difficult.

Notwithstanding these obstacles, developments in technology and data science are improving the power of EHR analysis. Techniques in natural language processing (NLP), for instance, make it possible to extract important information from unstructured data, like clinical narratives and doctor's notes. Enhanced data integration frameworks and interoperability standards make more thorough and coherent data analysis possible.

To summarize, EHR analysis for data science and analytics has enormous potential to improve patient outcomes, maximize operational effectiveness, promote public health programs, and advance medical research—all of which could completely revolutionize the healthcare industry. A greater understanding of health and disease is made possible by accessing and analyzing the enormous volumes of data found in EHRs, which eventually improves care and health outcomes. Continuous technological and data science advancements are increasing the potential for EHR analysis despite data privacy, quality, and interoperability obstacles. This suggests well for a future in which data-driven insights will be crucial to healthcare innovation and improvement.

Predictive Modeling for Patient Care

A revolutionary strategy in the healthcare sector is predictive modeling for patient care within data science and analytics. Predictive models try to predict future health outcomes using enormous volumes of historical and real-time data. This allows healthcare practitioners to provide more proactive, individualized, and effective care. This approach uses statistical methods, machine learning algorithms, and big data technologies to find trends and forecast patient health trajectories. This enhances clinical decision-making and patient outcomes in the long run.

The comprehensive data stored in Electronic Health Records (EHRs)—which include patient demographics, medical histories, test findings, imaging tests, treatment plans, and outcomes—lays the groundwork for predictive modeling in patient care. By evaluating this vast amount of data, predictive algorithms can determine risk factors and early warning indicators for various illnesses. Predictive analytics, for example, can predict the risk of readmissions to hospitals by looking at trends in prior hospitalizations, comorbidities, and patient behavior. With these models, healthcare professionals can take proactive steps to minimize readmissions, which enhances patient outcomes and lowers costs.

Managing chronic diseases is a critical area in which predictive modeling is used in patient care. Prolonged ailments, including diabetes, cardiovascular disease, and chronic obstructive pulmonary disease (COPD), necessitate ongoing observation and prompt treatment. Predictive models can examine patterns in patient health data to anticipate exacerbations or consequences, enabling early and focused therapies. Predictive models, for instance, can forecast blood glucose levels in diabetes patients based on historical readings, dietary preferences, and activity levels. This allows for the creation of individualized treatment programs to maintain ideal glucose control and avert problems.

Additionally, customized medicine—which adjusts medical care to each patient's unique needs—relies heavily on predictive modeling. By combining genetic and clinical data, predictive models can determine whether patients will likely respond to a specific treatment. Predictive models, for instance, can be used in oncology to assess treatment responses and genetic alterations to recommend the best chemotherapy regimen for a given patient. This customization increases patient happiness, decreases side effects, and improves therapy success.

Predictive modeling not only makes individual patient care better, but it also makes healthcare systems operate more efficiently. Clinics and hospitals can use predictive analytics to manage staff schedules better, allocate resources, and shorten patient wait times. Healthcare institutions can better plan for peak seasons and ensure that resources are allocated appropriately to meet patient demands by forecasting patient admission rates and lengths of stay. This promotes healthcare organizations' operational effectiveness and financial sustainability and improves patient care.

First comes the collecting and preprocessing of data, which is one of the most critical phases in the predictive modeling process. To create models that are trustworthy and accurate, high-quality data is necessary. After that, exploratory data analysis is performed on this data to find pertinent patterns and features. Feature engineering is critical in enhancing the model's predictive power when data scientists design new variables that capture relevant information. Predictive models are then constructed using a variety of machine learning algorithms, including logistic regression, decision trees, random forests, and neural networks. To ensure these models are reliable and applicable to a wide range of situations, they are trained on historical data and then cross-validated.

Predictive modeling has a bright future in patient care, but issues must be resolved. Given how sensitive health data is, data security and privacy are crucial. It is essential to follow laws like the Health Insurance Portability and Accountability Act (HIPAA) in the US. Furthermore, the completeness and quality of the underlying data determine the prediction models' accuracy and dependability. Overcoming interoperability obstacles is necessary when integrating data from several sources, such as genomic databases, wearable technology, and EHRs.

Interpretability of predictive models is another difficulty, especially for those built using sophisticated machine learning methods like deep learning. Clinicians must comprehend the process by which predictions are made to trust and act upon them. Thus, incorporating predictive analytics into clinical workflows requires creating interpretable models and offering concise justifications for the forecasts.

In summary, predictive modeling is a potent instrument in the data science and analytics toolbox that can improve patient outcomes, customize treatment regimens, and boost operational efficiency in the healthcare industry. Predictive models offer actionable insights that facilitate proactive and knowledgeable patient-care decision making by utilizing enormous volumes of health data and sophisticated analysis methodologies. Although there are still issues with data quality, privacy, and model interpretability, continuous technological and data science improvements are addressing these problems and clearing the path for predictive modeling to be used and integrated into healthcare on a larger scale.

Genomic Data Analysis

The study of genomic data has transformed the domain of data science and analytics by offering a significant understanding of the genetic underpinnings of both health and illness. Genomic data analysis looks at an organism's entire DNA sequence to comprehend genetic differences and how they affect biological processes. This strategy processes, analyzes, and interprets enormous volumes of genomic data, resulting in advances in personalized medicine, disease prevention, and pharmaceutical development. It does this by utilizing sophisticated computational techniques and big data analytics.

Developing high-throughput sequencing technologies, such as next-generation sequencing (NGS), has allowed for the economical and efficient production of large-scale genomic data. These technologies have made it possible to sequence complete transcriptomes, exomes, and genomes, resulting in significant and intricate data sets. Preprocessing and data gathering are the first two crucial processes in analyzing genomic data. Filtering low-quality reads and eliminating adaptor sequences are two examples of quality control processes necessary to address errors and biases frequently present in raw sequencing data. The data is guaranteed to be accurate and trustworthy for further analysis thanks to this preprocessing phase.

Following preprocessing, the data is mapped to a reference genome, which acts as a template for identifying genetic variants. By matching the sequencing reads to the reference genome, alignment methods enable the identification of structural changes, insertions and deletions (indels), and single nucleotide polymorphisms (SNPs). Understanding the genetic diversity among populations and the genetic underpinnings of diseases is based on these genetic variations. Variant calling is a popular process that finds and annotates these genomic variations. Tools like GATK (Genome Analysis Toolkit) and SAMtools are used for this purpose.

A significant use of genomic data analysis is in customized medicine, which adjusts a patient's course of care based on their unique genetic profile. By studying genomic data, healthcare professionals can predict patients' responses to therapies and detect genetic variants linked to particular diseases. Genomic data analysis, for instance, can identify mutations in cancer-related genes, such as BRCA1 and BRCA2, which are connected to a higher risk of ovarian and breast cancers. Knowing these genetic alterations enables the creation of individualized treatment programs, such as targeted treatments that target the precise molecular causes of a patient's cancer. Our strategy improves treatment efficacy and lowers side effects compared to conventional one-size-fits-all medications.

Determining genetic predispositions to different diseases is another important application of genomic data analysis. Researchers can find genetic risk factors for diseases like diabetes, neurological disorders, and cardiovascular diseases by analyzing the genomes of sizable populations. Genome-wide association studies, or GWAS, are famous for linking certain genetic variations to disease characteristics. To identify genetic markers that are more common in people with a specific disease, these investigations entail scanning the genomes of several people. The findings of GWAS can guide early interventions and preventive measures by offering essential insights into the genetic underpinnings of disease.

Furthermore, studying genetic data is essential to improving our comprehension of complicated features and behaviors. Scientists can create complete models of biological systems by combining genomic data with other omics data, such as transcriptomics, proteomics, and metabolomics. By shedding light on the complex relationships between genes, proteins, and metabolites, this integrated method—known as multi-omics analysis—offers a more comprehensive understanding of biological processes. Multi-omics analysis, for example, can show how genetic variants affect metabolic pathways and gene expression, contributing to disease development.

Examining genomic data is also essential to pharmacogenomics, which investigates how a person's genes influence how they respond to medications. Pharmacogenomics seeks to optimize drug therapy by comprehending the genetic elements influencing drug metabolism and efficacy so that patients receive the safest and most effective medicines according to their genetic profiles. By reducing adverse drug reactions and enhancing therapeutic results, this strategy opens the door to more individualized and successful treatment plans.

Genomic data analysis has several obstacles despite its revolutionary potential. Genomic data requires a great deal of computer power and sophisticated analytical techniques due to its sheer amount and complexity. Keeping genetic data private and secure is crucial since it includes sensitive information that needs to be shielded from unwanted access. Furthermore, because many genetic variants' functional implications are unknown, interpreting genomic data remains challenging. To overcome these obstacles and reach the full potential of genetic data analysis, more progress in bioinformatics, machine learning, and data integration is required.

To sum up, genomic data analysis provides deep insights into the genetic underpinnings of health and disease, making it a pillar of contemporary data science and analytics. Personalized medicine, disease prevention, and pharmaceutical development are made possible by genomic data analysis, which uses high-throughput sequencing technologies and sophisticated computer algorithms. While there are still obstacles to overcome, the field of genomic data analysis is becoming more and more capable thanks to continuous technological and bioinformatics improvements. This bodes well for when genetic data will be crucial to medical research and scientific understanding.

CHAPTER X

Financial Analytics

Fraud Detection

A crucial use of data science and analytics is fraud detection, which helps to protect financial systems, lower losses, and uphold confidence in several industries, including banking, insurance, e-commerce, and healthcare. Organizations can protect customers and businesses by utilizing machine learning algorithms, big data technology, and advanced data analytics approaches to detect and stop fraudulent activity in real time.

Studying enormous volumes of transactional data to find trends and abnormalities pointing to fraudulent activity forms the basis of fraud detection. Conventional approaches to detecting fraud depended on predetermined rules and manual evaluations, which, while somewhat successful, have limitations when identifying complex and dynamic fraud strategies. With the help of data science, fraud detection systems combine supervised and unsupervised learning to methods to increase precision and flexibility.

Supervised learning models are taught using past data labeled with instances of fraud and valid transactions. By finding patterns and correlations in the data, these models can identify the traits of fraudulent transactions. Neural networks, decision trees, random forests, and logistic regression are examples of algorithms that are often utilized. For instance, in the banking industry, supervised learning models can identify abnormal actions that differ from a customer's usual behavior by analyzing transaction amounts, frequencies, locations, and time stamps. These models enable real-time fraud detection and prevention because, once trained, they can forecast the probability of fraud in fresh transactions.

On the other hand, abnormalities in data are found by unsupervised learning, which does not require prior labeling. This method works exceptionally well for uncovering novel forms of fraud that were previously unknown. Using anomaly detection methods like isolation forests and autoencoders and clustering algorithms like DBSCAN and K-means is standard practice. These algorithms examine the data's natural structure to find anomalies or strange patterns that might point to fraud. Unsupervised learning, for instance, can be used to spot unusual claim patterns in the insurance sector that deviate considerably from the norm and may indicate fraud.

The application of ensemble learning, which integrates several models to enhance prediction performance, is another effective fraud detection strategy. Techniques like stacking, boosting, and bagging combine the advantages of several algorithms to provide a more reliable fraud detection system. The intricacies and fluctuations in transactional data are more effectively managed by ensemble models, yielding more precise and trustworthy fraud predictions.

High-performance computers and advanced analytics must be integrated to build real-time fraud detection systems. Thanks to streaming analytics solutions, transaction data may be continuously monitored and analyzed through the system. Data processing and analysis in real-time are frequently accomplished with the help of technologies like Apache Spark Streaming, Apache Flink, and Apache Kafka. These systems have millisecond fraud detection times, enabling quick responses such as transaction stopping, alert creation, or additional verification.

Contextual information and external data sources are beneficial additions to fraud detection systems. Social network analysis, for example, can help identify organized fraud rings by exposing links between bogus accounts. Furthermore, behavioral biometrics—such as mouse movements and keyboard dynamics—can improve the identification of fraudulent activity by examining user behavior patterns during online transactions.

There are still issues with fraud detection despite the advances. The imbalance in the dataset, where there are far fewer fraudulent transactions than valid ones, is one of the main problems. Models that are prejudiced and more prone to overlook fraud may result from this imbalance. To solve this problem, methods including under sampling, oversampling, and synthetic data synthesis (like SMOTE) are used. The dynamic and ever changing character of fraud schemes presents another difficulty. Fraudsters are always coming up with new ways to get around detection systems, meaning that models must be updated and improved. Responding to new fraud patterns is more accessible with continuous learning approaches, where models are regularly retrained with fresh data.

Data security and privacy are also crucial for detecting fraud. Because financial and personal data are sensitive, strict security measures must be taken to prevent breaches and unauthorized access. Maintaining data integrity and customer trust requires following laws like the Payment Card Industry Data Security Standard (PCI DSS) and the General Data Protection Regulation (GDPR).

To sum everything up, data science and analytics fraud detection is essential to safeguarding financial systems and minimizing economic losses. Modern fraud detection systems provide reliable and flexible ways to counteract fraudulent activity by utilizing supervised and unsupervised learning techniques, real-time analytics, and external data sources. Continuous advancements are improving the effectiveness of fraud detection in data science and technology despite persistent challenges like data imbalance, evolving fraud tactics, and concerns about data privacy. This means that organizations can stay ahead of fraudsters and maintain secure transactional environments.

Algorithmic Trading

Trading in the financial markets utilizing algorithms is known as algorithmic trading, sometimes called automated trading or algo trading. It is a sophisticated use of data science and analytics. This strategy uses computational power, statistical analysis, and intricate mathematical models to execute trades at unattainable frequencies and speeds for human traders. Algorithmic trading seeks to maximize profits by minimizing market effects, taking advantage of market inefficiencies, and optimizing the trading process through automation.

Trading algorithms, which are collections of guidelines and directives that specify when and how trades should be carried out, are the fundamental components of algorithmic trading. To find trading opportunities, these computers examine enormous market data, such as price, volume, and order book details. They verify methods and adjust parameters using historical data to ensure the algorithms are reliable and efficient in a range of market scenarios. Machine learning approaches like reinforcement learning and supervised learning are frequently used to hone these algorithms and raise their forecast accuracy.

Statistical arbitrage is a fundamental algorithmic trading strategy that involves taking advantage of price differences between connected financial assets. An example of statistical arbitrage is pairs trading, in which an algorithm finds two historically connected stocks and takes long and short bets in them when their prices diverge, betting that they will return to their previous relationship. Because the price differences in this technique are frequently tiny and transient, quick execution is necessary to profit from it. Therefore, high frequency trading capabilities are required.

Another popular algorithmic trading technique is market creation. Market makers consistently place buy and sell orders for a specific asset, which gives the market liquidity. Algorithms can optimize this process by dynamically modifying the bid-ask spread and order sizes in response to changes in the market, order flow, and inventory levels. By doing this, market makers control risk exposure while earning the bid-ask spread. Sophisticated risk management algorithms are needed for this technique to balance the inventory and prevent large losses from unfavorable price swings.

Algorithmic traders also frequently employ momentum trading, a technique predicated on the idea that assets with a track record of solid performance would continue to do so shortly. Using the persistence of price trends as leverage, algorithms identify trends and execute trades in the direction of the momentum. These algorithms seek to profit from long-term price movements by identifying entry and exit points using technical indicators like relative strength index (RSI) and moving averages.

Making predictions about market movements using machine learning models is another cutting-edge application of algorithmic trading. Large datasets, such as news stories, social media sentiment, economic indicators, and business fundamentals, can be analyzed by algorithms to produce trading signals. Algorithms can process and comprehend textual material thanks to natural language processing (NLP) techniques, allowing them to extract pertinent information that could impact asset prices. An algorithm could use sentiment analysis from financial news to forecast changes in stock prices and make trades depending on how news events are expected to affect prices.

An advanced technology infrastructure is necessary for the use of algorithmic trading. In particular, low-latency systems are essential for high-frequency trading (HFT) algorithms, which execute deals in microseconds. Co location services—where trading servers are positioned adjacent to exchange servers—are frequently utilized to reduce latency. Algorithmic trading platforms also need risk management and compliance tools to ensure that trading activities follow risk guidelines and legal requirements.

Algorithmic trading has several dangers and problems in addition to its benefits. One of the main challenges is the possibility that algorithms will act erratically in highly volatile markets, resulting in large financial losses. Faulty algorithmic trading is a common cause of flash crashes, which are brief but sharp drops in market value followed by sharp rises. Robust testing and validation techniques, such as scenario analysis and stress testing, are crucial to reducing these risks. Furthermore, because algorithmic trading is a competitive space, techniques may soon become outdated if competitors create better or more similar algorithms. To keep a competitive edge, research and development must be ongoing.

Furthermore, requests for tighter regulation of algorithmic trading operations are prompted by growing ethical and regulatory concerns regarding market stability and fairness.

Finally, algorithmic trading, which uses sophisticated algorithms and computing power to improve trading strategies and execute deals at previously unheard-of speeds, is a cutting-edge approach to the financial markets for data science and analytics. Algorithmic trading uses various data sources, risk management, and market inefficiencies to provide steady profits and improve market liquidity. However, strict testing, ongoing innovation, and adherence to regulatory norms are required to maintain ethical and sustainable trading methods in the financial industry due to the complexity and hazards involved with algorithmic trading.

Risk Management

Risk management is an important topic that requires careful consideration in data science and analytics. Organizations are increasingly depending on data-driven decision-making processes; thus, it is critical to recognize and reduce the risks involved. Fundamentally, risk management in data science and analytics is recognizing possible hazards, evaluating the potential consequences of those risks, and putting plans in place to reduce or eliminate them. Data security and privacy breaches are a significant danger in this field. The risk of malicious exploitation or unauthorized access to sensitive data is increasing due to its growth in collection and storage. Organizations must invest in robust security measures like encryption, access limits, and frequent audits to protect themselves from such attacks. Furthermore, compliance with data privacy rules like the CCPA and GDPR is essential to avoid legal ramifications.

Bias in algorithms and models is another issue with data science and analytics. Biased data or unreliable algorithms can produce inaccurate insights and judgments, supporting inequality and discrimination. To handle this issue, organizations must implement stringent validation and testing protocols to find and reduce biases in their data and models. Furthermore, encouraging inclusivity and diversity within data science teams might aid in lowering unconscious biases that arise during the creation and application of algorithms.

Moreover, the dependability of analytical findings may be jeopardized by insufficient data integrity and quality. Inaccurate, out-of-date, or complete data can result in accurate inferences and better decision-making. Organizations should implement procedures for data quality assurance and governance to reduce this risk. This entails ensuring data is relevant, correct, and consistent at every stage of its lifecycle—from collection to analysis. An efficient plan for data quality must include data lineage tracking, metadata management, and data cleansing techniques.

Scalability and performance issues in data science and analytics operations can carry concerns. Effective data processing and analysis may become more difficult for companies as datasets get bigger and computational demands rise. Problems with scalability might cause decision-making to take longer than expected and lower productivity. Organizations should invest in scalable infrastructure and use parallel processing strategies like cloud-based solutions and distributed computing to mitigate this risk. Furthermore, increasing the performance of algorithms and workflows can improve the effectiveness of data processing and analysis jobs.

Another important concern to consider is the lack of interpretability and openness in data science models. Black-box algorithms might make it difficult for stakeholders to comprehend and have faith in analytical insights since they provide no visibility into their decision making processes. Organizations should give top priority to developing clear and understandable models to reduce this risk. Model documentation, feature importance analysis, and model explanation techniques are a few of the strategies that can improve openness and encourage stakeholder participation.

To sum up, successful risk management is crucial to the long-term viability of data science and analytics projects. Organizations may maximize the benefits of data-driven decision-making while reducing potential drawbacks by recognizing and addressing risks such as data privacy breaches, algorithmic bias, problems with data quality, scalability limitations, and a lack of transparency. In addition to shielding enterprises from harm, putting strong risk management principles into practice promotes trust, accountability, and innovation in the data science and analytics community.

CHAPTER XI

Marketing Analytics

Customer Segmentation

An essential technique in data science and analytics is customer segmentation, which is breaking up a client base into discrete groups according to traits or actions they have in common. Businesses can more effectively target their marketing, provide individualized product recommendations, and improve customer experiences by using this segmentation to understand better their customers' requirements, preferences, and behaviors. Demographic segmentation is a popular customer segmentation method that divides consumers into groups according to demographic characteristics, including age, gender, income, education, and occupation. Businesses can customize their marketing messages and services to more effectively appeal to particular demographic groups by segmenting their consumer base based on their demographics. For instance, a clothes merchant would design distinct marketing campaigns for each to better cater to the interests and buying habits of various age groups and income brackets.

Psychographic segmentation is another popular approach to consumer segmentation that groups clients according to their values, interests, lifestyles, and personalities. Beyond demographic considerations, psychographic segmentation captures customer behavior's psychological and affective facets. Businesses can create more individualized marketing campaigns and product offerings that complement their customers' values and interests by learning about their psychographic profiles. For example, a health and wellness company may divide its clientele into groups according to their feelings about holistic living, exercise, and diet. This would enable the company to customize messaging and goods for each group.

Additionally, behavioral segmentation aims to group clients according to their usage habits, brand interactions, historical purchasing history, and other behavioral information. Businesses can find significant trends in consumer behavior and divide their clientele into groups according to factors like product preferences, buying patterns, degree of loyalty, and interaction with marketing efforts. Increasing engagement and loyalty enables companies to tailor their marketing campaigns, suggest pertinent items, and improve customer journeys. To offer individualized recommendations and promotional offers to each segment, an e-commerce platform could divide its client base into groups according to factors like average order value, product category preferences, and frequency of purchases.

Moreover, geographic segmentation splits clients according to their place of residence—nation, state, city, or neighborhood. By using geographic segmentation, businesses can consider geographical variations in competitive landscapes, economic situations, cultural norms, and preference patterns. Businesses can better serve clients' distinct needs and preferences in various regions by focusing their marketing strategy and product offers on these specific geographic segments. To better connect with local consumers, a restaurant chain, for example, can modify its menu selections and marketing strategies in response to local tastes and preferences.

Furthermore, by revealing hidden patterns and forecasting future behavior, cutting-edge segmentation strategies like predictive modeling and machine learning algorithms can improve customer segmentation efforts even more. Large amounts of consumer data can be analyzed by predictive models, which can then be used to find trends, correlations, and predictive elements that conventional segmentation techniques would have missed. By utilizing predictive analytics, businesses may discover high-value categories, predict client demands, and personalize interactions at scale. A subscription based business could use predictive modeling to spot at risk clients and take proactive measures to keep them around by focusing on retention.

Customer segmentation is a practical data science and analytics strategy that helps companies better understand and cater to their clientele. Businesses can customize their marketing tactics, product offers, and customer experiences to cater to various consumer segments' distinct requirements and preferences by segmenting their client base based on demographic, psychographic, behavioral, and geographic characteristics. In addition, sophisticated segmentation methods like machine learning algorithms and predictive modeling can improve segmentation efforts even further by revealing hidden patterns and forecasting future behavior. In the end, efficient customer segmentation enables companies to increase customer satisfaction, loyalty, and engagement, which boosts productivity and gives them a competitive edge.

Sentiment Analysis

Sentiment analysis is a practical data science and analytics technique. It entails taking subjective information from textual data and evaluating it to determine what sentiment or opinion is being communicated. Due to the widespread use of social media, online reviews, and consumer feedback, sentiment analysis has become more crucial for organizations to monitor brand perception, measure customer happiness, and comprehend public opinion. Sentiment analysis is frequently used in social media monitoring, where companies monitor mentions of their products or brands on various platforms to analyze sentiment trends and spot possible problems or possibilities. Businesses may learn a lot about their customers' thoughts, preferences, and sentiments about their brands, goods, and rivals by examining the tone of social media posts.

Furthermore, market research frequently uses sentiment analysis to examine consumer input via forums, surveys, and online reviews. Businesses may find important themes, feelings, and patterns in consumer feedback by automatically classifying and analyzing massive amounts of textual data. This enables them to evaluate their competitive posture, pinpoint areas for improvement, and make data-driven decisions. For instance, to prioritize upgrades and improve the overall guest experience, a hotel chain may utilize sentiment analysis to examine evaluations from past guests and find recurring problems or concerns about things like facilities, cleanliness, or service quality.

Furthermore, sentiment analysis is essential for reputation management and brand monitoring. Sentiment analysis is a valuable tool for businesses to monitor online brand mentions and evaluate consumer attitudes toward their brand across various platforms and demographics. Businesses may spot possible PR crises, recognize unfavorable sentiment early, and take proactive steps to rectify problems and minimize reputational harm by tracking sentiment changes over time. To preserve a positive brand image, a consumer electronics company, for example, can employ sentiment analysis to track online conversations about its products and promptly address customer concerns or unfavorable reviews.

In addition, news stories, social media posts, and other textual data are being analyzed for sentiment signals that could affect asset prices and market sentiment using sentiment analysis, which is becoming increasingly common in the financial markets. By examining the sentiment expressed in news headlines and social media conversations, traders and investors can obtain insights into market sentiment patterns, investor sentiment, and possible market-moving events. Sentiment analysis is helpful for traders and investors to evaluate market sentiment risk, spot sentiment-driven trading opportunities, and make better real-time investment decisions.

Furthermore, sentiment analysis has uses in customer service, politics, healthcare, and business and finance. Mood analysis in politics helps track attitudes toward political candidates, analyze public opinion on political issues, and estimate voter mood before elections. Sentiment analysis can assist in automating the classification and ranking of consumer inquiries according to sentiment in customer support, enabling companies to offer more effective and individualized customer care. Sentiment analysis can be used in the healthcare industry to evaluate patient comments, gauge patient happiness, and pinpoint areas where patient care and services need to be improved.

In short, sentiment analysis is a crucial data science and analytics technique that helps companies understand market trends, consumer sentiment, and public opinion by gleaning insightful information from textual data. Businesses can obtain practical insights to guide decision making, enhance customer experiences, and build a brand reputation by analyzing sentiment in news stories, social media posts, online reviews, and other textual data sources. Sentiment analysis is set to become a more significant factor in promoting innovation and corporate success across industries as natural language processing and machine learning progress.

Campaign Effectiveness

The goal of campaign effectiveness analysis is to assess the efficacy and influence of marketing campaigns across several channels and touchpoints, a critical use of data science and analytics in marketing and advertising. Businesses can optimize campaign plans, realize maximum return on investment (ROI), and obtain crucial insights into the efficacy of their marketing endeavors by utilizing data-driven techniques. Measuring key performance indicators (KPIs), including conversion rates, click-through rates, engagement metrics, and return on ad spend (ROAS), is an integral part of campaign effectiveness analysis. By monitoring these KPIs over time and across various marketing platforms, companies may evaluate the campaign's effectiveness and pinpoint areas for development.

Furthermore, attribution modeling is crucial to campaign performance research since it enables companies to link particular marketing touchpoints and channels along the customer journey to sales and conversions. Businesses can better allocate marketing resources and maximize campaign effectiveness by using attribution models, which show the relative contributions of each marketing channel and touchpoint to conversions and sales. By examining attribution data, businesses may determine which marketing channels have the most significant impact and allocate resources appropriately to optimize return on investment.

Furthermore, segmentation analysis contributes significantly to the study of campaign effectiveness by dividing up the client base according to their demographics, behaviors, preferences, and levels of engagement. Businesses can discover high-value client segments, target particular segments with offers and marketing messages, and increase overall campaign efficacy by evaluating campaign performance across various customer segments. For example, an e-commerce retailer can examine campaign results across different age groups or geographical areas to determine which segments have the highest conversion rates and return on investment.

A/B testing and experimentation are also crucial methods for analyzing campaign efficacy since they enable companies to test various campaign components, messaging alterations, and creative assets and identify the ones that produce the most significant outcomes. Through controlled experimentation and post-change analysis of essential data, firms can pinpoint winning methods, maximize campaign performance, and enhance marketing efficacy over an extended period. By repeatedly improving marketing plans based on empirical evidence, A/B testing can assist firms in making data driven decisions and avoiding costly mistakes.

Furthermore, by projecting future campaign success, client behavior, and development potential, predictive analytics can improve the analysis of campaign efficacy. Businesses can create predictive models to foresee the effects of future ads, improve targeting and segmentation tactics, and more efficiently deploy resources by utilizing past campaign data and customer insights. Businesses may reduce risks, maximize the success of their marketing campaigns, and anticipate potential campaign hazards with predictive analytics.

To sum things up, analyzing campaign performance is an essential use of data science and analytics that helps companies gauge, refine, and optimize the results of their advertising efforts. Utilizing data-driven strategies like segmentation analysis, A/B testing, attribution modeling, KPI tracking, and predictive analytics, businesses may uncover areas for development, obtain insightful knowledge about campaign effectiveness, and make well informed decisions that will propel their marketing initiatives. Campaign effectiveness analysis is evolving due to the growing amount of data available and advanced analytics technology. This helps organizations stay ahead of the competition and meet their marketing goals in today's ever-changing digital world.

CHAPTER XII

Social Media and Web Analytics

Analyzing Social Media Data

Businesses can gain essential insights from the massive volume of information created on social media platforms by using data science and analytics to analyze social media data. With billions of users globally interacting via social media, social media has developed into a wealth of data for sentiment research, brand perception, market trends, and consumer behavior studies. An essential component of social media data analysis involves keeping an eye on brand mentions, conversations, and sentiment on various platforms. Businesses may spot possible problems, respond to consumer feedback, and efficiently manage brand reputation by monitoring mentions of their brand or products. This gives them essential insights into client preferences, opinions, and sentiments towards their brand.

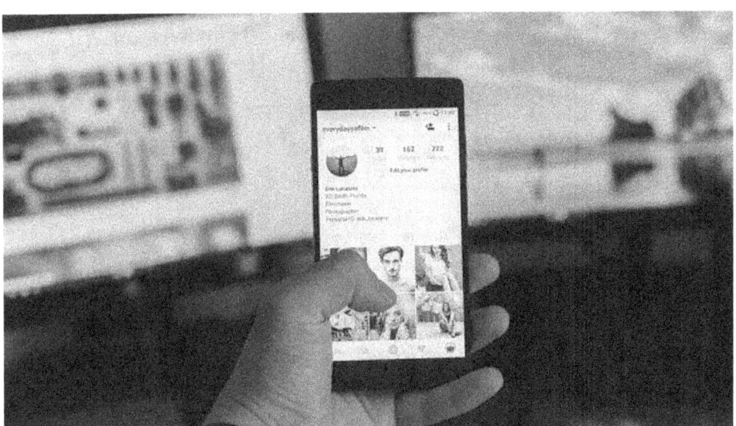

Social media data research also helps companies pinpoint hot subjects and new trends among their target market.

Real-time monitoring of hashtags, trending topics, and viral material allows organizations to remain current on consumer preferences, industry trends, and competitive dynamics. This enables businesses to seize opportunities, predict changes in the market, and modify their marketing strategy as necessary to keep ahead of the competition. For instance, a clothing retailer might use social media data analysis to pinpoint current fashion trends and adjust their product lines and advertising strategies to suit customer tastes.

Social media data analysis can also offer insightful information about targeting and audience segmentation. Businesses may divide their audience into discrete categories and customize their marketing messages and offers to more effectively appeal to each group by examining social media users' demographic data, interests, habits, and engagement metrics. This allows companies to provide their target audience with more individualized and pertinent information, which raises engagement, conversion rates, and return on investment. For example, by analyzing social media data, a travel agency might tailor its marketing strategies to target traveler segments interested in luxury travel, adventure tourism, or family trips.

Additionally, by determining the kinds of content that resonate best with the target audience, social media data research can help optimize and shape content strategy. Businesses can learn more about the efficacy of various content formats, themes, and publishing times by examining engagement indicators like likes, shares, comments, and click-through rates. Companies may increase the reach and effect of their content on social media platforms, improve their content strategy, and produce more exciting material. To help guide their content creation strategy, food brands may, for instance, examine social media analytics to see which recipe videos or food trends receive the most engagement.

Additionally, sentiment analysis helps analyze social media data, allowing companies to comprehend brand impressions, public opinion, and sentiment patterns. Businesses may spot potential PR problems, identify positive and negative sentiment patterns, and take proactive steps to manage brand reputation by evaluating the sentiment of social media posts, comments, and mentions. Businesses can use sentiment analysis to measure customer satisfaction, pinpoint areas for development, and make data-driven choices that will improve the customer experience in general. Sentiment analysis, for instance, can be used by a telecom firm to monitor consumer opinions of its goods and services and pinpoint common problems or pain areas that require attention.

In conclusion, social media data analysis is an essential use of data science and analytics that gives companies insightful knowledge about sentiment analysis, market trends, customer behavior, and brand impressions. Businesses may use social media data to guide marketing plans, improve brand reputation, and propel business success in the modern digital era by tracking brand mentions, spotting new trends, audience segmentation, content strategy optimization, and sentiment analysis. Businesses that use social media data analysis to their advantage are better positioned to satisfy their target audience's changing requirements and preferences and remain competitive in the face of the ever-increasing volume and complexity of social media data.

Web Traffic Analysis

A fundamental use of data science and analytics, web traffic analysis gives organizations essential insights into how people use their websites. Businesses may learn how visitors interact with their websites, pinpoint areas for development, and enhance the user experience to increase engagement, conversion, and retention by monitoring web traffic statistics. Monitoring and tracking key performance indicators (KPIs) such as website traffic, page views, bounce rates, session duration, and conversion rates are crucial to web traffic analysis. Businesses can evaluate the success of their website in drawing in and keeping visitors, spot any bottlenecks or problems, and make data-driven decisions to enhance website performance by tracking these metrics over time and across various segments.

Moreover, by examining how users engage with various pages, services, and content on their websites, web traffic analysis helps organizations better comprehend user behavior and preferences. Businesses can learn more about how visitors interact with their website, which pages or content are most popular, and where users drop off or leave by monitoring user navigation pathways, click patterns, and scroll behavior. This enables companies to spot chances to enhance calls-to-action, content arrangement, and navigation to raise user engagement and conversion rates. To determine which product features or photos have the highest conversion rates, an online shop may track user behavior on product pages and adjust how the products are presented.

Web traffic analysis also helps with content design and optimization by revealing the kinds of content website users are most interested in reading. Businesses may determine popular content subjects, forms, and themes that draw in and engage users by examining metrics like page views, time on page, and social shares. This enables companies to produce more interesting and pertinent content, increase organic traffic to their website, and better match their content strategy with user interests and preferences. To help guide future content development efforts, a digital marketing agency might examine blog post-performance data to see which subjects or formats bring in the most readers and interactions.

Web traffic research also offers essential insights into audience targeting and segmentation by examining website users' device types, demographics, geographic regions, and referral sources. Businesses may enhance the comprehension of their target demographic, customize offerings and marketing messages for various segments, and maximize ad targeting and personalization by dividing website visitors into discrete groups. This enables companies to raise engagement and conversion rates, enhance the relevance and efficacy of their marketing activities, and promote corporate expansion. To discover regions with the highest concentration of potential clients, a software company could monitor website traffic by geographic location and then focus marketing efforts in those areas.

Furthermore, through spotting chances to raise a website's exposure and ranks in search engine results pages (SERPs), web traffic research is essential to search engine optimization (SEO). Businesses can find high potential keywords and subjects to target, optimize website content and metadata, and enhance overall website performance in organic search by evaluating organic search traffic, keyword ranks, and search queries. This enables companies to raise their online presence and brand awareness, draw in more qualified leads, and grow their organic traffic. An online store might examine search volume and rankings to find long-tail keywords with little competition and high search volume, then tailor landing pages and product descriptions to fit those terms.

Simply put, traffic analysis is an essential use of data science and analytics that helps companies understand user behavior, improve the performance of their websites, and increase engagement, conversion, and retention. Businesses can increase the efficacy of their website and meet their marketing goals by monitoring key performance indicators, examining user behavior and preferences, refining content strategy, segmenting audience traffic, and optimizing search engines. Due to the ever-increasing volume and complexity of web traffic data, businesses that use web traffic analysis are better positioned to stay competitive, draw more customers, and expand their online presence and revenue in today's digital world.

Trends and Sentiment Analysis

An organization's ability to understand market dynamics, consumer behavior, and brand impression is greatly enhanced by trends and sentiment analysis, which are essential for data science and analytics. Using trend analysis, organizations can anticipate future developments, comprehend emerging trends, and make well-informed decisions by seeing patterns, changes, and shifts in data throughout time. Businesses may predict market trends, spot opportunities, and modify their strategy to stay ahead of the competition by examining past data and finding recurrent patterns. Retailers can, for instance, analyze sales data to spot seasonal patterns and then modify marketing campaigns and inventory levels to take advantage of these periods of high demand.

In contrast, sentiment analysis employs textual data to extract and analyze subjective information to ascertain sentiment or opinion. Businesses can learn about customer happiness, brand perception, and public opinion by examining the sentiment found in customer reviews, social media posts, and other textual sources. Using sentiment analysis, businesses better understand consumers' perceptions of their goods, services, and brands. This knowledge helps them find areas for development, respond to customer complaints, and efficiently manage their reputation. For example, hotels might use review data from past visitors to determine general satisfaction levels and pinpoint areas where facilities or service quality needs to be improved.

By combining trend and sentiment analysis, businesses can thoroughly grasp consumer mood and market dynamics. Companies can better understand the variables influencing consumer behavior and preferences by establishing a correlation between sentiment movements and market trends. Retailers could examine sentiment trends surrounding particular product categories to learn how shifts in customer perception affect sales results and modify their marketing plans accordingly. Similarly, financial institutions can use social media and news item sentiment trends analysis to predict changes in the market and assess investor mood.

Additionally, trend and mood analysis can assist companies in recognizing new opportunities as well as possible hazards. Businesses may proactively respond to shifting market conditions, reduce risks, and seize new possibilities by observing sentiment trends and spotting fluctuations in customer mood. For instance, to measure consumer reaction to new product releases or marketing campaigns and make necessary adjustments to maximize performance, businesses may examine sentiment patterns in the industry. Similarly, investors can examine sentiment patterns in financial markets to spot possible hazards or investment opportunities and modify their portfolios appropriately.

Moreover, trend and sentiment analysis are essential for reputation management and brand monitoring.

Businesses may evaluate brand image, spot any PR disasters, and take proactive steps to efficiently manage brand reputation by observing sentiment patterns. Brand mentions across various media. Businesses may monitor shifts in public opinion, spot bad sentiment early, and handle client complaints before they get out of hand using sentiment analysis. Companies may employ sentiment analysis to track news stories and social media mentions to spot possible reputational hazards and take appropriate action to safeguard their brand's image.

To wrap things up, trend and sentiment analysis are crucial data science and analytics techniques that give companies insightful knowledge about customer behavior, brand perception, and market dynamics. Businesses can forecast market developments, spot new possibilities, and reduce risks by tracking patterns over time and comparing them with sentiment trends. Moreover, sentiment research enables companies to successfully manage brand reputation, respond to client issues, and comprehend customer sentiment. Businesses that use trend and sentiment analysis are better positioned to make educated decisions, stay competitive, and drive corporate success in today's dynamic and competitive business climate because of data's ever-increasing volume and complexity.

CHAPTER XIII

Case Study 1

Problem Statement

To identify, analyze, and solve complex problems using data-driven methodologies, creating a problem statement is an essential first step in any data science and analytics project. A clear and concise problem statement gives the project's whole lifecycle direction and clarity by articulating the particular opportunity or difficulty it seeks to address. Knowing the problem's background and extent is common in creating a problem statement. This entails figuring out the relevant stakeholders, comprehending their aims and objectives, and drawing the limits of the problem domain. The problem statement guarantees that the project stays focused and aligned with stakeholder demands and expectations by clearly defining boundaries and objectives.

Additionally, a well-written problem statement puts the issue in quantifiable terms, making it possible to evaluate outcomes and solutions objectively. This entails determining the metrics or key performance indicators (KPIs) that will be used to evaluate the project's success. The problem statement establishes a foundation for assessing the efficacy of data-driven solutions and quantifying their influence on business outcomes by specifying specific and quantifiable objectives. A problem statement for a sales forecasting project could include KPIs like forecast accuracy, revenue growth, and inventory management to provide a clear baseline to evaluate the forecasting model's performance.

A substantial problem statement also highlights the problem's importance and relevance, emphasizing its impact on stakeholders and the organization as a whole and the reasons it must be addressed. To do this, the problem context must be carefully examined, along with any consequences for revenue creation, customer happiness, corporate operations, or risk management. The problem statement ensures that resources are allocated correctly and that the project has the necessary support and prioritization by clearly outlining the business case for addressing the problem and gaining buy-in from stakeholders and decision-makers.

A well-defined problem statement also lists the resources and data sources that can be used to solve the issue, along with any potential limits or restrictions that can affect the project. To do this, a data inventory must be carried out to locate pertinent data sources, data availability and quality must be evaluated, and any gaps or restrictions in the data must be found and potentially fixed. The issue statement guides decisions on data collecting, processing, and analysis methodologies by providing an upfront understanding of the data landscape and resource constraints. It also helps set realistic expectations for what can be accomplished within the project scope.

A thorough problem statement also considers techniques for risk mitigation as well as potential risks and uncertainties that could influence the project. This entails performing a risk assessment to identify potential roadblocks, such as problems with data quality, technical difficulties, or resistance from stakeholders, and creating backup plans to deal with these concerns in advance. The problem statement lowers project delays and interruptions and raises the possibility of project success by foreseeing and resolving potential hazards early on.

Developing a problem statement is an essential initial step in any data science and analytics project. It gives a clear and concise explanation of the issue that needs to be solved, the goals that need to be met, and the strategy that should be used. The basis of a well-defined issue statement ensures that the project stays focused, aligned with stakeholder needs, and positioned for success across the entire project lifecycle. Effective problem-solving and data-driven decision-making are made possible by the problem statement, which outlines the problem's significance and relevance, defines measurable goals, identifies data sources and resources, and addresses potential risks and uncertainties.

Approach and Methodology

The technique and methodology used in data science and analytics are crucial factors that determine a project's efficacy and success. A straightforward approach specifies the procedures and methods to be followed, and a methodology offers a structure for carrying out those procedures in an orderly and exacting way. The six-phase CRISP-DM (Cross-Industry Standard Process for Data Mining) methodology is a popular approach to data science projects. It comprises six stages: business understanding, data understanding, data preparation, modeling, assessment, and deployment. This methodology offers an organized framework for working on data science projects. It begins with comprehending the business problem and the stakeholders' goals, then moves on to gathering, cleaning, and preparing data, modeling and analysis, assessing the performance of the models, and putting the solution into use.

Also, agile and iterative approaches—prioritizing adaptability, teamwork, and continual improvement—are frequently used in data science and analytics initiatives. Scrum and Kanban are examples of agile methods that help teams prioritize work according to risk and value, adjust to changing requirements, and produce incremental results in brief, iterative cycles. Agile approaches assist in speeding up project delivery, reducing risks, and raising stakeholder satisfaction by segmenting the project into smaller, more manageable tasks and providing value often. Through quick hypothesis testing, outcomes evaluation, and method adjustments based on feedback, teams using this iterative approach can also experiment and learn.

Furthermore, depending on the nature of the issue and the data at hand, the approach for data science and analytics initiatives usually combines quantitative and qualitative techniques. Structured data is analyzed quantitatively to find patterns, correlations, and trends using statistical analysis, machine learning, and predictive modeling. These methods help companies make data-driven decisions, streamline internal operations, and extract valuable insights from massive amounts of data. However, unstructured data —text, photos, and audio—is analyzed using qualitative methods like text mining, sentiment analysis, and content analysis to gain essential insights and comprehend people's thoughts, feelings, and behaviors.

Additionally, a multidisciplinary approach is frequently used in the methodology for data science and analytics projects, utilizing knowledge and skills from various fields, including statistics, computer science, mathematics, and domain-specific experience. Data scientists, statisticians, domain experts, and business stakeholders collaborate in collaborative teams to establish project goals, locate data sources, create analytical models, and interpret outcomes. Multidisciplinary teams can tackle complicated challenges more successfully, consider many points of view, and ensure that the solutions developed are technically solid and aligned with business goals by combining multiple perspectives and talents.

To guarantee data quality, integrity, and security throughout the project lifetime, robust data management and governance procedures are also a part of the methodology for data science and analytics initiatives. This entails setting data quality assurance procedures, creating data governance frameworks, and complying with legal obligations like GDPR and HIPAA. Together with data warehouses, data lakes, and ETL (extract, transform, load) pipelines, data management strategies also encompass data collecting, storage, integration, and processing. Companies can rely on the outcomes of their studies and make well-informed decisions by upholding data security and integrity.

Furthermore, during the project, communication, cooperation, and transparency are emphasized as critical components of the approach for data science and analytics projects. Good communication guarantees that all parties involved in a project agree regarding its goals, course, and results and proactively handle any possible problems or hazards. Team members who collaborate are more likely to be creative and innovative and to share knowledge, which helps them to use one another's skills and abilities better to solve challenging situations. Transparency guarantees that facts support judgments and that interested parties know the procedures, presumptions, and constraints that underlie the analyses and findings.

In summary, a data science and analytics project's approach and methodology are essential to its success because they offer a defined framework for setting goals, carrying out activities, and giving value to stakeholders. Businesses can optimize the efficacy and influence of their data science endeavors by embracing approaches like CRISP-DM and agile, utilizing quantitative and qualitative methods, forming interdisciplinary teams, putting strong data management and governance procedures in place, and emphasizing openness, cooperation, and communication. In today's quickly changing business world, companies that adopt a systematic and rigorous approach to data science and analytics will be better able to drive innovation, make data-driven decisions, and gain a competitive edge. This is because data volume and complexity are only going to increase.

Results and Insights

The output of data science and analytics projects are results and insights, which give stakeholders helpful information and practical suggestions. Analyzing data, using statistical and machine learning methods, and interpreting the results is necessary to produce relevant results and insights that inform corporate choices and actions. A vital component of providing outcomes and understandings is guaranteeing the examination's precision, dependability, and legitimacy. This entails checking assumptions, ensuring data quality, and extensively validating analytical models to guarantee reliable and solid outcomes. Data scientists can ensure that the insights produced are dependable and valuable by following the best data analysis and interpretation practices. This will also help them gain the respect and trust of stakeholders.

Furthermore, efficient communication and decision making depend on the data and insights being presented clearly, succinctly, and engagingly. Charts, graphs, and dashboards are examples of data visualization techniques that can be used to show complex data and analytical conclusions in a visually appealing and understandable way. Thanks to visualizations, stakeholders are better able to make decisions based on the insights provided when they have immediate access to critical patterns, trends, and linkages in the data. Additionally, the results can be contextualized, essential discoveries can be highlighted, and the consequences for operations and corporate strategy can be communicated using storytelling approaches. Data scientists can include stakeholders, convey the importance of the findings, and spur action by telling a story with their discoveries.

Furthermore, comprehending the needs and preferences of stakeholders in addition to the company context and objectives is necessary to give meaningful insights. By aligning analysis with business goals and priorities, data scientists may guarantee that the insights produced are pertinent and significant, tackling particular opportunities or issues the company encounters. This entails collecting input from stakeholders at every stage of the project, working closely with them, and incorporating their ideas into the process of analysis and interpretation. Data scientists may ensure that the insights provided match stakeholders' needs and expectations and have the best chance of producing profitable business outcomes by incorporating them early and frequently.

Furthermore, delving beyond descriptive analytics to find more profound patterns, correlations, and causal links in the data is necessary for understanding findings and insights. Predictive modeling, clustering, and segmentation are examples of advanced analytical approaches that can be used to find hidden patterns and trends, project future results, and divide the target population into groups according to shared traits or behaviors. Data scientists may proactively identify opportunities and dangers and predict future trends using predictive analytics. This gives stakeholders a competitive edge and allows them to take preventive action. Additionally, by identifying the underlying causes of observable trends or phenomena, root cause analysis can assist stakeholders in addressing the underlying problems and putting focused solutions in place to achieve desired results.

Delivering results and insights entails combining information from many data sources and analytical methods to present a complete picture of the issue or opportunity. To improve the analysis and give more context, this may entail integrating internal and external data, including market research, customer data, and industry benchmarking. By combining varied data sources and perspectives, data scientists can comprehensively understand the issue, recognize recurring patterns, and formulate practical solutions that cater to the interests of various stakeholders. Furthermore, performing scenario planning and sensitivity analysis can assist in determining the viability of the insights and assessing the possible effects of multiple assumptions or scenarios on company outcomes.

To sum everything up, producing results and insights is a crucial component of data science and analytics projects, giving stakeholders helpful knowledge and practical suggestions to influence business choices. Data scientists can provide: Insights that significantly impact the organization by guaranteeing the validity, reliability, and accuracy of the analysis. Presenting the results understandably and engagingly. Coordinating the analysis with stakeholder needs and business goals. Utilizing cutting-edge analytical techniques. Synthesizing findings from various data sources. Due to the ever-increasing volume and complexity of data, organizations that invest in data science and analytics capabilities are better positioned to make informed decisions, streamline business processes, and gain a competitive advantage in today's data-driven world.

CHAPTER XIV

Case Study 2

Problem Statement

As the first stage in defining the project's goals, approach, and scope, creating a thorough issue statement is essential to every data science and analytics initiative. The problem statement acts as a road map, assisting in directing the project toward significant results and guaranteeing that it is in line with the requirements and expectations of stakeholders. Fundamentally, a problem statement clarifies the particular opportunity or difficulty that the project seeks to address, offering guidance and direction across the project's whole lifecycle. Data scientists may concentrate their efforts on solving the correct problem and providing actionable insights that add value to the enterprise by explicitly identifying the problem statement up front.

On top of that, a well-defined issue statement starts with a complete comprehension of the goals and business environment, guaranteeing that the project is based on demands and priorities relevant to the real world. This entails interacting with stakeholders to ascertain needs, pinpoint problems, and establish the project's success criteria. Data scientists may guarantee the generated insights are pertinent, significant, and actionable by ensuring that the issue description is in line with corporate objectives and stakeholder expectations. In a retail context, the problem statement might focus on streamlining inventory management to lower stockouts and raise customer happiness, which aligns with the organization's primary objective of increasing sales and profitability.

Furthermore, during the project lifecycle, a substantial problem statement helps manage expectations and prevent scope creep by precisely defining the limits and extent of the problem space. This entails identifying the crucial factors, data sources, and limitations that will affect the analysis and choice-making procedure. Data scientists can concentrate their efforts on the most critical parts of the problem and avoid unnecessary details or diversions by setting clear limits up front. When creating a predictive model to predict customer churn, for instance, the problem statement can clearly define the scope of the analysis by stating the relevant input variables (such as customer demographics and purchase history) and the desired output (such as the probability of churn within a given period).

A well-written problem description also specifies the target audience or stakeholders who stand to gain from the project's findings. This entails being aware of the information requirements and decision-making procedures of essential parties, like operations teams, marketing managers, and company executives. Data scientists can make sure that the insights produced apply to the target audience and are actionable by customizing the problem statement to meet the demands of particular stakeholders. In healthcare, for instance, the issue statement can center on forecasting patient readmissions to assist hospital managers in better-allocating resources and enhancing patient outcomes, meeting the requirements of both patients and healthcare providers.

A thorough problem statement also provides transparency and accountability throughout the project lifecycle by outlining the analytical approach and technique that will be utilized to address the issue. To evaluate the data and produce insights, this entails selecting the data sources, analytical methods, and modeling frameworks that will be used. Data scientists may make sure that the technique is exacting, repeatable, and compliant with industry best practices in data science and analytics by outlining the analytical approach in advance. For instance, the problem statement for creating a predictive model for fraud detection may outline the features of engineering methods, data preparation procedures, and model assessment metrics that will be utilized to gauge the efficacy and performance of the model.

A clear problem definition also identifies any obstacles, unknowns, and constraints that might affect the analysis and decision-making process. This entails carrying out a risk assessment to pinpoint any roadblocks, including problems with data quality, technological limitations, or stakeholder resistance, and creating mitigation plans to deal with these difficulties in advance. Data scientists can reduce project delays and disruptions and raise the chance of project success by foreseeing and addressing potential hazards early on. For instance, the problem statement for sentiment analysis of social media data may recognize the noise and ambiguity present in textual data and provide methods for preprocessing and filtering the information to increase sentiment analysis accuracy.

To sum up, developing a thorough problem statement is an essential first step in any data science and analytics project. It gives a clear and straightforward explanation of the issue to be solved, the goals to be met, and the strategy to be used. In addition to defining the extent and boundaries of the problem space, identifying the target audience, outlining the analytical approach and technique, and acknowledging potential problems and limitations, a well-defined problem statement provides alignment with stakeholder needs and expectations. Data scientists can create a substantial problem statement and set themselves up for success by devoting time and energy upfront to produce insights that are useful to the company.

Approach and Methodology

The approach and technique employed in data science and analytics function as a guide for those navigating the intricate process of deriving insights from data. They consist of an organized system of methods, instruments, and procedures that direct the implementation of data- driven initiatives from start to finish. In addition to guaranteeing the efficacy, precision, and dependability of studies, a robust approach and methodology are essential for producing actionable insights that promote wise decision-making and positive business outcomes.

The CRISP-DM (Cross-Industry Standard Process for Data Mining) methodology, which consists of six phases—business understanding, data understanding, data preparation, modeling, assessment, and deployment—is a popular approach to data science and analytics initiatives. This methodology begins with comprehending the business problem and stakeholder objectives and offers an organized foundation for taking on data science projects. After that, data understanding entails obtaining, examining, and evaluating data to learn more about its composition, caliber, and applicability to the issue. Cleaning, preprocessing, and transforming data to prepare it for analysis is known as data preparation, and modeling is the process of choosing, creating, and assessing analytical models to find patterns, correlations, and trends in the data. The deployment phase entails incorporating the analytical solution into operational systems and processes to reap the advantages. In contrast, the assessment phase evaluates the models' performance and confirms that they effectively solve the business challenge.

In addition, data science and analytics projects frequently use an agile and iterative methodology emphasizing adaptability, teamwork, and continual development. Scrum and Kanban are examples of agile approaches that help teams prioritize work according to risk and value, adjust to changing requirements, and produce incremental results in brief, iterative cycles. Agile approaches assist in speeding up project delivery, reducing risks, and raising stakeholder satisfaction by segmenting the project into smaller, more manageable tasks and providing value often. Through quick hypothesis testing, outcomes evaluation, and method adjustments based on feedback, teams using this iterative approach can also experiment and learn.

Additionally, depending on the nature of the problem and the data available, the approach for data science and analytics projects usually combines quantitative and qualitative techniques. Structured data is analyzed quantitatively to find patterns, correlations, and trends using statistical analysis, machine learning, and predictive modeling. These methods help companies make data-driven decisions, streamline internal operations, and extract valuable insights from massive amounts of data. However, unstructured data—text, photos, and audio—is analyzed using qualitative methods like text mining, sentiment analysis, and content analysis to gain essential insights and comprehend people's thoughts, feelings, and behaviors.

Furthermore, a multidisciplinary approach is frequently used in the methodology for data science and analytics projects, utilizing knowledge and skills from various fields, including statistics, computer science, mathematics, and domain-specific experience. Data scientists, statisticians, domain experts, and business stakeholders collaborate in collaborative teams to establish project goals, locate data sources, create analytical models, and interpret outcomes. Multidisciplinary teams can tackle complicated challenges more successfully, consider many points of view, and ensure that the solutions developed are technically solid and aligned with business goals by combining multiple perspectives and talents.

Furthermore, data governance and management are essential parts of the methodology for data science and analytics projects, guaranteeing data security, quality, and integrity throughout the project's lifetime. This entails setting data quality assurance procedures, creating data governance frameworks, and complying with legal obligations like GDPR and HIPAA. Together with data warehouses, data lakes, and ETL (extract, transform, load) pipelines, data management strategies also encompass data collecting, storage, integration, and processing. Businesses can rely on the outcomes of their studies and make well-informed decisions by upholding data security and integrity.

To ensure stakeholders are involved, informed, and in sync throughout the project lifecycle, data science and analytics projects must incorporate good communication, collaboration, and transparency as fundamental components of their methodology. Teams can ensure that the project stays on course and that any possible problems or concerns are handled early on by creating clear communication channels, providing progress reports, and asking for stakeholder input. Team members who collaborate are more likely to be creative and innovative and to share knowledge, which helps them to use one another's skills and abilities better to solve challenging situations. Transparency guarantees that facts support judgments and that interested parties know the procedures, presumptions, and constraints underlying the analyses and findings.

To sum everything up, the methodology and strategy for data science and analytics projects offer an organized framework for setting goals, carrying out activities, and providing value to stakeholders. Businesses can optimize the efficacy and influence of their data science endeavors by embracing approaches like CRISP-DM and agile, utilizing quantitative and qualitative methods, forming interdisciplinary teams, putting strong data management and governance procedures in place, and emphasizing openness, cooperation, and communication. Organizations that adopt a systematic and rigorous approach to data science and analytics are better positioned to drive innovation, make data-driven decisions, and gain a competitive advantage in today's data-driven world due to the ever-increasing volume and complexity of data.

Results and Insights

The ultimate goal of data science and analytics efforts is results and insights, which are the observable results that promote successful business operations and well- informed decision-making. Results and insights are two different concepts in data science initiatives. Results are the conclusions drawn from data analysis, and insights are the practical knowledge that follows from those conclusions. When combined, outcomes and insights enable businesses to discover the untapped potential of their data, comprehend their business and clients better, and spot areas for innovation and improvement.

Getting valuable insights from data analysis is one of the main goals of data science and analytics initiatives. Various statistical, machine learning, and data mining approaches are applied to big and complicated datasets to identify patterns, trends, and correlations. For instance, data scientists may employ clustering techniques to divide the client base according to purchasing patterns or regression analysis to pinpoint variables influencing consumer response rates in a marketing campaign analysis. Using sophisticated analytical methods, data scientists can find essential insights that need to be visible using conventional approaches. This helps firms make better decisions and achieve better results.

Additionally, businesses can leverage the actionable intelligence derived from data analysis to enhance client experiences, streamline corporate procedures, and spur innovation and growth. For instance, customer segmentation analysis data may identify distinct consumer personas with particular requirements and preferences, allowing businesses to better target their product offers and marketing messages in each category. Similarly, companies can prevent equipment breakdowns using information from predictive maintenance analysis. This proactive maintenance approach reduces downtime and increases operational effectiveness. Organizations can achieve sustained growth and success and obtain a competitive advantage in their marketplaces by converting data into actionable insights.

Moreover, data scientists and stakeholders throughout the enterprise must effectively communicate and collaborate to produce actionable insights. Data scientists need to be skilled communicators and knowledgeable in data analytic methodologies to communicate their findings to audiences who could be more technical effectively. This could entail producing reports, dashboards, and visualizations that succinctly and easily convey the most important findings and suggestions. Furthermore, working with stakeholders guarantees that the insights produced are pertinent and aligned with corporate goals, empowering firms to effect significant change and realize their goals.

Also, iterative exploration and experimentation are frequently included in concluding data, as data scientists improve their analysis and hypotheses in response to fresh discoveries and input from stakeholders. Through constant learning and adaptation to shifting consumer preferences and market situations, this iterative strategy helps firms spur continuous innovation and progress. To increase the precision and applicability of recommendations over time, data scientists might regularly enhance their algorithms in a product recommendation system depending on user input and engagement metrics. Organizations can maintain flexibility and responsiveness to changing market conditions and business requirements by adopting an iterative approach to data analysis.

Furthermore, the supply of insights marks the start of a cycle of ongoing development and refinement rather than the conclusion of the data science and analytics process. Companies must keep a close eye on how their insights affect business results and modify their tactics and strategies as necessary. This could entail collecting feedback from stakeholders to pinpoint areas that need improvement, running A/B tests to evaluate various methods, and monitoring key performance indicators (KPIs) and metrics to assess the efficacy of solutions that have been put into place. In today's quickly changing business environment, organizations can foster continuous improvement and achieve long-term success by embracing a data-driven approach to innovation and decision-making.

To sum it up, data science and analytics are vital because they yield outcomes and insights that give businesses the knowledge and understanding they need to make wise decisions and succeed as a corporation. Organizations may optimize operations, enhance customer experiences, spur growth, and foster innovation by utilizing sophisticated analytical approaches to extract valuable insights from data. The attainment of targeted results and the delivery of actionable insights are contingent upon effective communication, collaboration, and iteration. Organizations may fully utilize their data and obtain a competitive advantage in today's data-driven world by adopting a data-driven strategy for innovation and decision-making.

CHAPTER XV

Case Study 3

Problem Statement

The foundation of any successful data science and analytics endeavor is the creation of a clear problem statement. It defines the precise opportunity or challenges that the project seeks to address, acts as a compass, and establishes the course for the entire analytical process. A clear and concise problem statement summarizes the main points of the issue, including its goals, importance, and scope. It also acts as a guide for the analytical process that will be used.

A substantial problem definition begins, first and foremost, with a deep comprehension of the stakeholder objectives and the business context. Data scientists can identify the underlying business demands, obstacles, and possibilities that motivate the project's start by interacting with stakeholders. During this first stage, requirements-collecting meetings, workshops, and stakeholder interviews are held to obtain essential insights and match project goals with organizational objectives. In the context of e-commerce, the problem statement can be about optimizing product recommendations to improve consumer engagement and boost sales, which is in line with the company's primary objective, which is to maximize revenue and profitability.

Furthermore, a well-written problem statement clearly defines the parameters and extent of the problem area, giving the analytical efforts direction and clarity. This entails identifying the crucial factors, data sources, and limitations that will affect the analysis and choice-making procedure. Data scientists can guarantee that the project stays manageable and that efforts are focused on solving the most critical parts of the issue by setting clear boundaries up front. For example, the problem statement should clearly define the desired output (churn probability within a given period) and the pertinent input variables (such as customer demographics and purchase history) to create a predictive model for customer churn.

A practical problem description also specifies the stakeholders or target audience that will gain from the project's insights. This entails being aware of the information requirements and decision-making procedures of essential parties, like operations teams, marketing managers, and company executives. Data scientists can make sure that the insights produced are pertinent and valuable to the target audience by customizing the issue statement to meet the demands of particular stakeholders. In healthcare, for instance, the issue statement can center on forecasting patient readmissions to assist hospital managers in better allocating resources and enhancing patient outcomes, meeting the requirements of both patients and healthcare providers.

A thorough problem statement also provides transparency and accountability throughout the project lifecycle by outlining the analytical approach and technique that will be used to address the issue. To evaluate the data and produce insights, this entails identifying the modeling frameworks, analytical methods, and data sources. Data scientists may make sure that the technique is exacting, repeatable, and compliant with industry best practices in data science and analytics by outlining the analytical approach in advance. For instance, the problem statement for creating a predictive model for fraud detection may outline the features of engineering methods, data preparation procedures, and model assessment metrics that will be utilized to gauge the efficacy and performance of the model.

Furthermore, a clearly stated problem description recognizes any obstacles, doubts, and constraints that can affect the analysis and choice-making process. This entails carrying out a risk assessment to pinpoint any roadblocks, including problems with data quality, technological limitations, or stakeholder resistance, and creating mitigation plans to deal with these difficulties in advance. Data scientists can reduce project delays and disruptions and raise the chance of project success by foreseeing and addressing potential hazards early on. For instance, the problem statement for sentiment analysis of social media data may recognize the noise and ambiguity present in textual data and provide methods for preprocessing and filtering the information to increase sentiment analysis accuracy.

To sum things up, developing a clear and concise issue statement is an essential first step in any data science and analytics project. It outlines the goals to be met, the strategy to be employed, and the problem to be solved. In addition to defining the extent and boundaries of the problem space, identifying the target audience, outlining the analytical approach and technique, and acknowledging potential problems and limitations, a well defined problem statement provides alignment with stakeholder needs and expectations. Data researchers may create a substantial problem statement and set themselves up for success by devoting time and energy upfront to develop valuable insights for the company.

Approach and Methodology

Technique and approach are crucial elements in data science and analytics that direct the systematic and organized implementation of initiatives meant to extract insights from data. These elements give data scientists a road map describing the actions, methods, and resources used throughout the project lifecycle. A clearly defined approach and methodology ensure consistency, efficacy, and rigor in data analysis, producing significant insights that support both corporate success and well-informed decision-making.

Understanding the business environment and stakeholder goals is frequently the first step in the data science and analytics process. To develop the issue statement, choose key performance indicators (KPIs) and set project success criteria; this entails strong collaboration with stakeholders. Data scientists can ensure that the insights produced are pertinent and actionable, addressing particular opportunities or issues encountered by the company by coordinating the study with business goals and priorities. For instance, in a retail setting, the strategy might concentrate on streamlining inventory management to lower stockouts and raise customer happiness, which would align with the company's main objective, which is to maximize sales and profitability.

Furthermore, a standardized framework, such as the CRISP-DM (Cross-Industry Standard Process for Data Mining) methodology, is usually used while doing data science and analytics initiatives. The six stages of this methodology comprise the business understanding, data understanding, data preparation, modeling, evaluation, and deployment processes. Stakeholder identification, success criteria definition, and project aim clarification are all part of the business understanding phase. Gathering, examining, and evaluating data is part of the data understanding phase, which aims to provide insights about the data's quality, structure, and applicability to the current issue. Cleaning, preparing, and modifying the data to make it analytically ready are the main goals of the data preparation stage. The modeling process entails choosing, creating, and assessing analytical models to find patterns, correlations, and trends in the data. The models' performance is evaluated during the evaluation phase, and their suitability for solving the business challenge is confirmed. To fully reap the benefits of the analytical solution, the deployment phase culminates in integrating it into operational systems and procedures.

Additionally, data science and analytics initiatives frequently use an agile and iterative methodology to promote adaptability, teamwork, and ongoing development. Scrum and Kanban are examples of agile approaches that help teams prioritize work according to risk and value, adjust to changing requirements, and produce incremental results in brief, iterative cycles. Through quick hypothesis testing, outcomes evaluation, and method adjustments based on feedback, teams may experiment and learn using this iterative approach. Agile approaches assist in speeding up project delivery, reducing risks, and raising stakeholder satisfaction by segmenting the project into smaller, more manageable tasks and providing value often.

Furthermore, depending on the nature of the problem and the data available, the approach for data science and analytics projects usually combines quantitative and qualitative techniques. Structured data is analyzed quantitatively to find patterns, correlations, and trends using statistical analysis, machine learning, and predictive modeling. These methods help companies make data-driven decisions, streamline internal operations, and extract valuable insights from massive amounts of data. However, unstructured data—text, photos, and audio—is analyzed using qualitative methods like text mining, sentiment analysis, and content analysis to gain essential insights and comprehend people's thoughts, feelings, and behaviors.

Technique and approach play a crucial role in data science and analytics initiatives since they offer an organized framework for setting goals, carrying out activities, and giving value to stakeholders. Organizations can enhance the efficacy and impact of their data science programs by using approaches like CRISP-DM and agile, utilizing quantitative and qualitative techniques, and coordinating the analysis with stakeholder demands and business goals. Organizations that adopt a systematic and rigorous approach to data science and analytics are better positioned to drive innovation, make data-driven decisions, and gain a competitive advantage in today's data-driven world due to the ever-increasing volume and complexity of data.

Results and Insights

The culmination of data science and analytics efforts is results and insights, which are the concrete products that support successful corporate decision-making. Within the context of data science initiatives, results are the conclusions drawn from the data analysis, while insights are the useful information gleaned from those conclusions. When combined, outcomes and insights enable businesses to find areas for innovation and optimization, realize the full potential of their data, and better understand their clients and operations.

The search for significant outcomes from data analysis is at the heart of data science. This means analyzing large and complex datasets for patterns, trends, and correlations using a variety of statistical, machine learning, and data mining techniques. For example, data scientists in the finance industry might use time series analysis to spot market trends and project future stock values, or they might use clustering techniques to divide up the clientele into groups according to how they spend. Using the application of sophisticated analytical methods, data scientists uncover meaningful insights that might not be apparent using traditional approaches, helping firms make better decisions and achieve better results.

Moreover, data analysis provides firms with actionable intelligence that can be utilized to improve customer experiences, streamline operations, and foster innovation and growth. For instance, customer segmentation study data may reveal discrete consumer personas with specific requirements and preferences, enabling businesses to successfully customize their product offers and marketing tactics to each segment. Predictive maintenance analysis provides valuable data that can help firms anticipate equipment breakdowns and take proactive measures to minimize downtime and improve operational efficiency. Organizations can obtain a competitive advantage in their markets and design a course for long-term growth and success by converting data into actionable insights.

Furthermore, good communication and cooperation between data scientists and stakeholders within the company are essential to delivering meaningful insights. To effectively communicate their findings to non-technical audiences, data scientists must be proficient in data analytic techniques and communication. This could mean producing reports, dashboards, and visualizations that concisely convey essential findings and suggestions intelligibly and readably. Furthermore, working with stakeholders guarantees that the insights produced are pertinent and aligned with corporate goals, empowering firms to effect significant change and realize their goals.

Furthermore, iterative exploration and experimentation are frequently required in concluding data, as data scientists improve their analysis and hypotheses in response to fresh discoveries and input from stakeholders. Through constant learning and adaptation to shifting consumer preferences and market situations, this iterative strategy helps firms spur continuous innovation and progress. For instance, data scientists may continuously improve their algorithms in recommendation systems based on user input and engagement metrics to improve the relevancy and accuracy of recommendations over time. Organizations can maintain flexibility and responsiveness to changing market conditions and business requirements by adopting an iterative approach to data analysis.

To wrap it up, outcomes and discoveries are vital to data science and analytics because they provide businesses with the information and understanding required to make wise decisions and accomplish their goals. Organizations can optimize operations, enhance customer experiences, spur growth, and foster innovation by applying sophisticated analytical approaches to extract valuable insights from data. The attainment of targeted results and the delivery of actionable insights are contingent upon effective communication, collaboration, and iteration. Through the adoption of a data-driven strategy for innovation and decision-making, firms may fully utilize their data and obtain a competitive advantage in the current data-driven market.

CHAPTER XVI

Data Privacy and Security

Legal and Regulatory Issues

Organizations must negotiate legal and regulatory challenges in data science and analytics to assure compliance, reduce risks, and enforce ethical standards in data handling. Governments and regulatory agencies have been forced to establish laws and rules to protect people's rights and interests. Worries about privacy, security, and accountability have gained traction as data becomes more and more essential to company operations and decision-making.

The General Data Protection Regulation (GDPR) is a leading legislative framework that regulates data privacy and protection. It was enacted by the European Union (EU) in 2018. The General Data Protection Regulation (GDPR) imposes stringent guidelines on acquiring, handling, and retaining personal data. It also gives people more choice over the personal data they provide, and non-compliance carries significant penalties. Organizations that handle the data of EU citizens are required to get express consent before processing data, put safeguards in place to protect the security and integrity of the data, and give people the ability to access, update, and remove their data at any time. Due to the GDPR's extraterritorial reach, compliance with its obligations is essential everywhere that enterprises handle the data of EU citizens.

Comparably, state-by-state variations exist in data privacy laws in the United States, with California setting the standard with the California Consumer Privacy Act (CCPA). The California Consumer Privacy Act (CCPA), passed in 2018 and revised in 2020, gives citizens of California more control over their data. Some of these rights include the ability to request that their data be deleted, to know what information is being gathered about them, and to opt out of having their data sold. The CCPA applies to companies that fulfill specific requirements, such as managing the personal data of fifty thousand or more consumers, households, or devices or having an annual gross revenue of over $25 million.

Furthermore, maintaining patient privacy and protecting protected health information (PHI) in the healthcare industry depends heavily on compliance with the Health Insurance Portability and Accountability Act (HIPAA). HIPAA lays out strict guidelines for the confidentiality and security of PHI, requiring security measures to stop unwanted access, use, or disclosure of private patient information. Administrators, insurers, and clearinghouses for health information must put administrative, physical, and technical security measures in place to guarantee HIPAA compliance and reduce the possibility of data breaches or privacy violations.

Furthermore, there are particular ethical and legal issues in data science and analytics related to new technologies like artificial intelligence (AI) and machine learning (ML). The potential for algorithmic bias and the opaque nature of AI algorithms raises questions about accountability, transparency, and fairness in decision-making processes. Organizations must design AI and ML models that adhere to ethical standards, objectivity, and legal requirements, including the right to due process and the prohibition of discriminatory behaviors.

Furthermore, data breaches and cybersecurity threats can significantly threaten an organization's financial viability, legal liability, and reputation. Due to the increase in cyberattacks targeting sensitive data, organizations need to have strong cybersecurity measures in place to protect themselves from harmful actions, data theft, and unauthorized access. Organizations can reduce cybersecurity risks and show dedication to data security and privacy by adhering to industry standards like the Payment Card Industry Data Security Standard (PCI DSS) and the ISO/IEC 27001 framework.

In conclusion, data privacy, security, transparency, and ethical considerations are only a few of the many facets and constantly changing legal and regulatory issues in data science and analytics. Organizations may proactively solve these problems by establishing robust data governance frameworks, adhering to applicable rules and regulations, and maintaining ethical standards in gathering, processing, and using data. In the age of big data and analytics, companies can reduce risks, gain the trust of stakeholders, and promote responsible innovation by prioritizing legal and regulatory compliance.

Best Practices for Data Security

Organizations must negotiate legal and regulatory challenges in data science and analytics to assure compliance, reduce risks, and enforce ethical standards in data handling. Governments and regulatory agencies have been forced to establish laws and rules to protect people's rights and interests. Worries about privacy, security, and accountability have gained traction as data becomes more and more essential to company operations and decision-making.

The General Data Protection Regulation (GDPR) is a leading legislative framework that regulates data privacy and protection. It was enacted by the European Union (EU) in 2018. The General Data Protection Regulation (GDPR) imposes stringent guidelines on acquiring, handling, and retaining personal data. It also gives people more choice over the personal data they provide, and non-compliance carries significant penalties. Organizations that handle the data of EU citizens are required to get express consent before processing data, put safeguards in place to protect the security and integrity of the data, and give people the ability to access, update, and remove their data at any time. Due to the GDPR's extraterritorial reach, compliance with its obligations is essential everywhere that enterprises handle the data of EU citizens.

Comparably, state-by-state variations exist in data privacy laws in the United States, with California setting the standard with the California Consumer Privacy Act (CCPA). The California Consumer Privacy Act (CCPA), passed in 2018 and revised in 2020, gives citizens of California more control over their data. Some of these rights include the ability to request that their data be deleted, to know what information is being gathered about them, and to opt out of having their data sold. The CCPA applies to companies that fulfill specific requirements, such as managing the personal data of fifty thousand or more consumers, households, or devices or having an annual gross revenue of over $25 million.

Furthermore, maintaining patient privacy and protecting protected health information (PHI) in the healthcare industry depends heavily on compliance with the Health Insurance Portability and Accountability Act (HIPAA). HIPAA lays out strict guidelines for the confidentiality and security of PHI, requiring security measures to stop unwanted access, use, or disclosure of private patient information. Administrators, insurers, and clearinghouses for health information must put administrative, physical, and technical security measures in place to guarantee HIPAA compliance and reduce the possibility of data breaches or privacy violations.

Furthermore, there are particular ethical and legal issues in data science and analytics related to new technologies like artificial intelligence (AI) and machine learning (ML). The potential for algorithmic bias and the opaque nature of AI algorithms raise questions about accountability, transparency, and fairness in decision-making processes. Organizations must design AI and ML models that adhere to ethical standards, objectivity, and legal requirements, including the right to due process and the prohibition of discriminatory behaviors.

Furthermore, significant dangers exist to an organization's financial viability, legal liability, and reputation associated with data breaches and cybersecurity threats. Organizations need strong cybersecurity measures to protect themselves from harmful actions, data theft, and unauthorized access due to the increase in cyberattacks that target sensitive data. Organizations can reduce cybersecurity risks and show dedication to data security and privacy by adhering to industry standards like the Payment Card Industry Data Security Standard (PCI DSS) and the ISO/IEC 27001 framework.

In conclusion, data privacy, security, transparency, and ethical considerations are only a few of the many facets and constantly changing legal and regulatory issues in data science and analytics. Organizations may proactively solve these problems by establishing robust data governance frameworks, adhering to applicable rules and regulations, and maintaining ethical standards in gathering, processing, and using data. In the age of big data and analytics, companies can reduce risks, gain the trust of stakeholders, and promote responsible innovation by prioritizing legal and regulatory compliance.

CHAPTER XVII
Ethical Considerations in Data Science

Bias and Fairness in Data Analysis

The ethics, validity, and accuracy of analytical insights are shaped by the fairness and bias of data analysis, which are essential factors in data science and analytics. Organizations are becoming increasingly dependent on data-driven decision-making, which increases the possibility of bias seeping into data analysis procedures and creating accountability, transparency, and fairness issues. Maintaining the legitimacy and trustworthiness of data-driven processes, minimizing social and ethical concerns, and guaranteeing equitable results depend on addressing bias and advancing fairness in data analysis.

The inherent biases in the data itself are one of the leading causes of bias in data analysis. Sample biases, selection biases, or data collection techniques can all lead to the manifestation of historical biases, systematic disparities, and societal prejudices in datasets. Biased sample approaches, for instance, have the potential to alter reality by excessively including or excluding particular demographic groups. Analyses that fail to consider the potential for bias perpetuation and reinforcement can also result from collecting data from sources that mirror past inequities, including criminal justice records or loan approval data.

Furthermore, biased training data can teach machine learning models patterns and relationships that result in biased predictions and judgments. This is known as algorithmic bias. This problem may arise from biased assumptions ingrained in the model's architecture or models trained on data reflecting social prejudices. For example, if biased training data is not adequately mitigated, it may lead to discriminatory outcomes in face recognition, recruiting, or predictive policing algorithms. Because it can exacerbate and maintain structural inequities, exacerbate social injustices, and strengthen discrimination against marginalized groups, algorithmic bias presents severe ethical problems.

Fairness and bias reduction in data analysis necessitate a multipronged strategy that includes data gathering, preprocessing, modeling, and assessment. Critically assessing the representativeness and variety of the data used for analysis is one crucial tactic. Another is actively reducing biases using data augmentation, sample plans, or anonymization. Additionally, algorithmic bias can be lessened, and equitable outcomes can be promoted by utilizing fairness-aware algorithms and methodologies like fairness constraints, bias mitigation algorithms, or fairness-aware assessment metrics.

Moreover, detecting and reducing bias in data analysis procedures depends on accountability and transparency. Organizations must have open procedures so interested parties may comprehend data gathering, processing, and application in decision-making. This entails recording the preprocessing stages, modeling assumptions, evaluation criteria, and data sources so interested parties can judge the accuracy and equity of the analytical insights. Furthermore, implementing accountability systems like impartial audits, fairness impact analyses, or bias review boards can support efforts to mitigate prejudice and promote equitable and fair decision-making.

Additionally, encouraging inclusivity and diversity in data science teams helps lessen bias and promote a more comprehensive and representative method of data analysis. The diverse teams' perspectives, experiences, and insights allow for more thorough and nuanced evaluations considering a more extensive range of factors. Organizations can lessen the possibility of prejudice and advance justice in data analysis procedures by cultivating a culture of diversity, equity, and inclusion within data science teams.

To sum everything up, fairness and bias are essential factors in data analysis, affecting analytical findings' validity, accuracy, and moral implications. A proactive, multimodal strategy that includes data collection, preprocessing, modeling, and evaluation phases is needed to address bias. Organizations may reduce bias, advance justice, and preserve the credibility of data driven decision-making by encouraging openness, accountability, and diversity in their data analysis procedures. Setting fairness as a top priority in data analysis is morally required and crucial for guaranteeing fair results and building confidence in data-driven procedures.

Ethical Decision-Making Frameworks

Frameworks for ethical decision-making give data scientists and analytics professionals the critical direction they need to resolve complex moral problems and guarantee the ethical and responsible use of data. Maintaining moral principles and values is essential to building trust, protecting privacy, and reducing social and ethical hazards in a time when data-driven technologies have a tremendous impact on people, societies, and economies. An organized method for assessing the moral implications of data science and analytics initiatives, spotting any dangers and effects, and directing moral decision-making procedures is provided by ethical decision-making frameworks.

The Fair Information Practice Principles are one well known paradigm for making ethical decisions in data science and analytics (FIPPs). FIPPs, which privacy activists and legislators formulated, delineate a fundamental framework for the just and moral handling of personal data. These principles include minimization of data (gathering only the information required for the intended purpose), purpose specification (defining the purposes for which data is collected and used), accountability (ensuring accountability for compliance with data protection laws and regulations), and transparency (giving individuals clear and understandable information about data practices). Data science practitioners may respect people's right to privacy, advance accountability and openness, and foster confidence in data-driven procedures by following the FIPPs.

Furthermore, a thorough framework for the creation and application of moral AI is offered by the Responsible AI Framework, which groups like the Partnership on AI created. The framework guides enterprises in the appropriate use of AI technologies by encompassing concepts like accountability, transparency, justice, and privacy. For instance, the accountability principle highlights the necessity of distinct lines of accountability and monitoring in AI research and deployment. In contrast, the fairness principle stresses the significance of guaranteeing that AI systems are free from bias and discrimination. Organizations may reduce ethical risks, ensure the moral application of AI technology, and foster confidence in AI-driven decision-making by implementing the Responsible AI Framework.

Additionally, the Ethical Data usage Framework offers a formal method for assessing the ethical implications of data usage in study and practice, which scholars and ethicists have developed. Principles like beneficence— maximizing benefits and minimizing harms to people and society— justice—ensuring fairness and equity in the use and distribution of data—and autonomy—respecting people's right to control their data and make decisions about its use—are all included in the framework. Organizations can evaluate the ethical implications of data use, recognize potential risks and damages, and take necessary action to address moral issues and uphold ethical standards by using the Ethical Data Use Framework.

Additionally, companies can traverse ethical problems in data science and analytics initiatives with the help of practical guidance provided by ethical decision-making frameworks like the Data Ethics Decision-Making Framework created by the Data Ethics Commission. Organizations can use the framework, which consists of a set of questions and considerations, to assess the ethical implications of using data. These include possible effects on people and society, dangers of harm and discrimination, and steps to reduce risks and encourage ethical behavior. Organizations can maintain ethical standards and guarantee the responsible and ethical use of data in their operations and decision-making processes by methodically assessing ethical factors and making informed judgments.

To sum up, ethical decision-making frameworks offer crucial direction for data science and analytics experts to handle moral dilemmas and guarantee the ethical and responsible use of data. In the age of big data and analytics, organizations may reduce ethical risks, foster confidence in data-driven processes, and maintain ethical standards by abiding by values like openness, fairness, accountability, and respect for autonomy. In a data-driven society, prioritizing ethical decision-making is not only morally required but also crucial for fostering social good, protecting privacy, and establishing confidence.

CHAPTER XVIII

Practical Challenges and Solutions

Dealing with Big Data

Big data in data science and analytics is both an opportunity and a problem for companies looking to use data's enormous potential to spur innovation and insights. Big data, defined by its volume, velocity, and variety, presents businesses with never-before-seen chances to find previously undiscovered patterns, trends, and insights. Extensive data management, processing, and analysis require specialized tools, methodologies, and infrastructure to solve the inherent obstacles given by their magnitude and complexity.

Handling the sheer volume of big data, which can overwhelm conventional data management systems and infrastructure, is one of the main issues. Large datasets that are larger than the capacity of traditional databases and storage systems are produced when big data is produced quickly from various sources, including sensors, social media, and transactional systems. Organizations must invest in distributed and scalable data processing and storage solutions, such as cloud-based data warehouses and the Hadoop Distributed File System (HDFS), to meet this challenge. These systems must also be scalable enough to handle increasing data volumes.

Furthermore, the velocity of big data refers to the rate at which information is created, gathered, and processed in real-time or almost real-time. IoT devices, social media feeds, and financial transactions are examples of streaming data sources that generate data at a high velocity. As a result, enterprises must deploy real-time data processing and analytics capabilities to extract relevant insights quickly. Organizations can ingest, process, and analyze streaming data in real-time thanks to technologies like Apache Kafka and Apache Storm, which facilitate prompt decision-making and responsiveness to shifting market conditions.

Big data is also distinguished by its diversity, including semi-structured, unstructured, and structured data from various sources and formats. Big data requires a wide range of data kinds and formats beyond traditional relational databases' capabilities. As a result, specific tools and technologies are needed for data integration, cleansing, and transformation. Organizations can analyze various datasets efficiently thanks to the robust data processing frameworks offered by technologies like Apache Spark and Apache Flink, which support a broad range of data types and formats. Big data also presents data integrity, consistency, and quality issues since it might contain errors, biases, or inconsistencies that affect the dependability and accuracy of analytical insights. These issues arise from the massive amounts of data gathered from many sources. Organizations must have data quality management procedures and instruments to handle these issues and guarantee that the data is accurate, dependable, and clean. Standardizing data formats and removing errors may entail data cleansing, deduplication, and normalizing procedures. Additionally, data validation and quality checks may be used to find and fix abnormalities and inconsistencies in the data.

Big data also creates privacy and security issues since businesses need to ensure that private information is sufficiently shielded from misuse, unwanted access, and breaches. Organizations are under increasing legal pressure to protect sensitive and personal data due to the rise in data breaches and privacy laws like the CCPA and GDPR. Protecting sensitive data and upholding regulatory compliance necessitate strong security measures like encryption, access limits, and data anonymization.

To sum it up, enterprises looking to utilize data science and analytics fully have both possibilities and challenges when working with extensive data. Big data presents never-before-seen possibilities for novel discoveries and creative thinking. Still, to handle, process, and analyze big data efficiently, specific tools, methods, and infrastructure are needed to meet the challenges that come with it. Organizations can fully realize the potential of big data and create value in today's data-driven world by investing in scalable and distributed data storage and processing solutions, putting real-time data processing and analytics capabilities into place, addressing privacy and data quality concerns, and ensuring regulatory requirements are met.

Overcoming Resource Limitations

Organizations hoping to use data science and analytics effectively to promote insights and innovation must overcome resource constraints. Budgetary, human, or technological resource constraints can be major obstacles for businesses looking to use data to its fullest advantage to accomplish their goals. Organizations may, however, overcome these obstacles and unleash the revolutionary potential of data science and analytics by implementing strategic initiatives and effectively utilizing the resources that are now accessible.

Budgetary restrictions are a typical resource limitation in data science and analytics activities. These limitations hinder an organization's capacity to invest in state-of-the art technologies, recruit highly qualified personnel, or get superior data sources. Organizations might take a staged approach to data science projects, focusing on quick wins that provide noticeable benefits in the near term and prioritizing projects with the highest prospective return on investment to get around budgetary constraints. Organizations can also investigate more affordable options like crowdsourcing data, cloud-based services, and open-source software to reduce initial costs and optimize the benefits of data science projects.

Furthermore, a significant resource constraint for businesses looking to develop their data science and analytics skills is a need for more personnel. It can be difficult for companies to find and keep top talent because there is a constant demand for data science specialists with experience in fields like predictive analytics, machine learning, and data visualization. Organizations might engage in reskilling and upskilling current staff members through training programs, workshops, and online courses to improve data science competencies internally to address the workforce gap. Organizations can also access a wider talent pool and tap into emerging talent pipelines by collaborating with academic institutions, industry groups, and professional networks.

Furthermore, firms may find it easier to grow data science and analytics programs with restricted access to technical infrastructure, such as processing power and data storage. Organizations can use cloud computing platforms, like Google Cloud Platform (GCP), Microsoft Azure, and Amazon Web Services (AWS), to get on demand storage and computing power without making a sizable upfront investment in hardware and infrastructure. This allows them to get around infrastructure constraints. Scalability, flexibility, and cost effectiveness are provided by cloud-based services, which enable businesses to adjust their resource allocation to match changing demand and maximize resource efficiency.

Additionally, organizations hoping to gain insights from data science and analytics programs face significant data availability and quality obstacles. The accuracy and dependability of analytical insights can be hampered by incomplete, inconsistent, or poor-quality data, resulting in less-than-ideal decision-making outcomes. Organizations can use data governance frameworks and quality management procedures to guarantee that data is accurate, dependable, and clean to address data availability and quality issues. This may entail data cleansing, standardization, and enrichment approaches to increase data quality and consistency. It may also comprise data integration and aggregation tactics to combine several data sources into a comprehensive dataset.

In addition, companies can get beyond resource constraints by cultivating an innovative, collaborative, and continuous improvement culture inside the company. Organizations can use the varied perspectives and experiences of business, IT, and data science teams to foster cross-functional collaboration. This approach can aid in surmounting obstacles, recognizing prospects, and promoting innovation in data science and analytics endeavors. To overcome resource constraints and accomplish desired results, organizations can also promote a culture of experimentation and learning by motivating teams to take measured risks, test theories, and refine solutions.

In summary, enterprises looking to leverage data science and analytics' revolutionary potential to spur insights and innovation must overcome resource constraints. Organizations can overcome budgetary restrictions, talent shortages, infrastructure limitations, and data quality challenges to fully realize the potential of data driven decision-making by implementing strategic approaches, effectively utilizing available resources, and cultivating a culture of innovation and collaboration. Organizations can use the opportunities provided by data science and analytics to meet their strategic goals and promote sustainable growth and success by overcoming resource constraints and adopting the appropriate mentality, tools, and approaches.

Continuous Learning and Adaptation

The fields of data science and analytics are based on the fundamental ideas of continuous learning and adaptation, which help organizations keep up with the rapidly changing methods, best practices, and technology in the field of data-driven innovation. In the current era, where new data sources, technologies, and methodologies are emerging at a quick rate and data quantities are rising exponentially, companies must be able to continuously adapt and learn to stay competitive and maximize the value of their data assets.

The speed at which technology is developing is one of the leading forces behind data science and analytics' constant learning and adaptability. The way businesses gather, handle, and analyze data is being completely transformed by new technologies like artificial intelligence (AI), machine learning (ML), and big data platforms. These technologies present never-before-seen chances to get new insights and spur innovation. Data science experts can strengthen their analytical skills, streamline decision making procedures, and seize new chances for value generation by keeping current on developing technologies and trends.

Additionally, because data science and analytics are dynamic fields, practitioners must constantly modify their knowledge and skill sets to stay up to date with shifting market trends and company needs. Data scientists must develop new skills, broaden their knowledge base, and hone their analytical methods to keep up with their organizations' ever-changing demands. In an increasingly competitive environment, data science professionals can stay ahead of the curve and relevant by participating in continuous learning efforts like training programs, workshops, online certifications. courses, and professional

Furthermore, due to the iterative nature of data science projects, ongoing learning and adaptation are required throughout the project. Experimentation, hypothesis testing, and iterative model and algorithm modification based on feedback and insights from data analysis are common components of data science initiatives. Teams that use an iterative approach to data science projects can improve the efficacy and impact of their studies by learning from past mistakes, refining solutions, and adjusting their strategy in response to new data and evolving requirements.

Furthermore, because data science and analytics are multidisciplinary fields, professionals working in these fields must develop a wide range of abilities, including technical proficiency, domain knowledge, and soft skills like critical thinking, problem-solving, and communication. Programs for continuous learning that encourage interdisciplinary cooperation and information exchange give data scientists the ability to use a variety of viewpoints and specialties to tackle difficult problems and spark creativity in data-driven decision-making.

Companies also need to cultivate a culture of ongoing learning and adaptation to develop an atmosphere that rewards experimentation, creativity, and information sharing. Organizations can assist their teams in learning continuously, adapting to change, and driving innovation in data science and analytics initiatives by investing in professional development, giving access to learning resources and training opportunities, and cultivating a collaborative and supportive work environment.

In conclusion, organizations may stay ahead of the curve and maximize the value of their data assets by adhering to the fundamental principles of continuous learning and adaptation in data science and analytics. In today's data-driven world, companies may employ data science and analytics to create insights, make informed decisions, and accomplish strategic objectives by embracing evolving technologies, learning new skills, and cultivating a culture of experimentation and innovation. Organizations can position themselves for success in the increasingly competitive and dynamic field of data-driven innovation by committing to ongoing learning and adaptation.

CONCLUSION

The book "Data Science and Analytics: Transforming Raw Data into Actionable Insights: A Comprehensive Guide" thoroughly examines the concepts, procedures, and uses of this field of study. The book provides readers with a detailed understanding of how unprocessed data can be converted into insightful understandings that support creativity and decision-making by skillfully bridging theoretical ideas with real-world applications. It addresses crucial concerns, including bias, fairness, ethical considerations, and a wide range of topics like data collection, preprocessing, modeling, and visualization. By using a thorough approach, readers are guaranteed to understand not just the technical parts of the work but also its broader context and ramifications. Through the integration of case studies, practical examples, and hands-on activities, the book provides practitioners with the essential tools and expertise required to navigate the intricate data landscape effectively. Ultimately, this manual is a priceless tool for anybody wishing to use data science and analytics to produce valuable insights and add value to their respective industries.